HannaH

Same Both Ways

Hannah Rose

Written in collaboration with
Susan and David Mitchell

Pen Press

First published in Great Britain by Pen Press

All paper used in the printing of this book has been made from wood grown in managed, sustainable forests.

ISBN13: 978-1-78003-594-9

Printed and bound in the UK
Pen Press is an imprint of
Indepenpress Publishing Limited
25 Eastern Place
Brighton
BN2 1GJ

A catalogue record of this book is available from

the British Library

Cover design by Claire Spinks - based on an original idea
by Gillian Mitchell

Dedicated to Mum, Dad, Jessica, Naomi and Grandparents Lou, Ruth and Frances who have always been there for me

'I just want you to know that out of all the people I have treated over the years you have shown the most courage and been the most inspiring because you have been the first person I have treated on a ventilator who has gone back to work. You've shown true spirit.'

Consultant, Southport Spinal Injuries Unit

'Hannah's had so many barriers to overcome, more than any person should have to deal with, yet she is still very much the same person. I think that's amazing.'

Lizzy (friend)

'I don't see Hannah as a disabled person. To me she is Hannah Rose, my friend. Hannah now sees herself as someone who CAN.'

Tia (friend and work colleague)

Acknowledgements

Thanks to Sue and Dave for doing a brilliant job with the book and to all the many people who have helped me along my journey.

CONTENTS

INTRODUCTION

I looked out across an audience of about 80 health professionals who seemed to be hanging on to my every word as I addressed them. I was in the St John's Church Hall in Hartford, my home village in Cheshire. It was July 2012. Early nerves had gone and I was warming to my task with every sentence. The more I gained in confidence, the more I came away from my carefully prepared notes. I described my life, stage by stage, and illustrated my words with photographs on a screen behind me.

I came to the end and looked across the hall in amazement as the audience rose as one to give me a standing ovation! It was the most wonderful feeling that I think I have ever experienced, and the applause which rang out around the room confirmed something very important to me – that my story had moved them.

There was an opportunity to answer questions, the second of which came from a dear friend, also disabled. He asked me, 'What's your next step, Hannah?' I talked about setting up home on my own.

His follow-up comment shocked me. My friend turned to the audience and said to them: 'Everybody, I want you to know how much Hannah has inspired me over the last few years.' He was close to tears and so was I.

CHAPTER ONE

Something for Grandpa Lou

'... a therapeutic process.'

I've been trying to write this book for some time. Why?

Under normal circumstances I wouldn't have been considering writing a book about my life at the age of 28. I would be working in relative anonymity, enjoying holidays and time with my friends and family. I would be at the gym once every week or so and looking ahead to starting my own family. That's the kind of life I had pictured in my mind as I was growing up. I had no great plans or expectations. It's certainly not the stuff that books are made of.

Now I have a story worth sharing with you.

It was Grandpa Lou who kept encouraging me to write things down before I forgot them. That was the starting point. Another early inspiration was my friend Celia who also suggested that I record my memories and make a book out of them.

I had no idea how difficult it would prove to be. Using my own technology, I would dictate my words only to find that the predictive text often spelt them out quite differently. I was spending far too much time correcting things and getting so frustrated with myself.

Then, in December 2011, we had a visit from Dave and Sue Mitchell. The three of us had some time together and I told them about the book that I wanted to write. When I mentioned how difficult it was proving to be, Dave reassured me that he had a solution. On his next visit he produced a tiny digital voice recorder, pressed a button and placed the black gadget carefully on my still body. Then he told me to do what, for Hannah Rose, is the easiest thing in the world – start talking! It took a few moments to get used to hearing myself on tape but then I was away! Suddenly, the whole process was so much easier and the story spilled out. I've always nattered along at nineteen to the dozen and not having to worry about writing everything down was brilliant! In fact, the problem was shutting me up! I've always had that problem – both as an able-bodied and as a disabled person. You ask those who are nearest and dearest to me. They'll tell you!

Dave and Sue were able to prompt me, guide me and put some order into my many thoughts. In short, they took the project by the scruff of the neck. We were interrupted by telephone calls, the front door bell, the need for a brew and my dog Bella's whining noises, but nothing got in our way. Everything was stored in the little black box. Dave then had the thankless task of editing all my ramblings! I apologised over and over again for meandering from one subject to another but all that Sue kept saying was: 'Don't worry, Dave will sort it out!'

Although the book's existence remained our secret it soon became obvious that so much more could be achieved by bringing other people in, and that was what we started to do. I've been able to add extra pieces to my own personal jigsaw as family and friends have had their say. Listening to others has shown me how much I had forgotten and missed because of my state of mind at the time and the effect of medication. It has, therefore, been a therapeutic process both for me and for them and has helped me come to terms with how my life has turned upside down. I hope that you, the readers, might take something from this book for yourselves and, who knows, it may help you cope with issues in your own lives. If it does, then it has been worth the time and effort.

I feel like I'm doing something proactive by writing this book. It's a well-known fact in my house that I'm always talking about doing things but never getting round to them! Well, now I have. I hope that you find it as interesting to read as I have found it to write and many thanks to Sue and Dave for making it possible.

CHAPTER TWO
A Walk with Bella

'There is many a time when I wish I could turn back the clock.'

It's Friday 13th today, unlucky for some! Not for me! It is January 2012 and almost exactly a month since Sue and Dave first got involved with this book. They are beside me now and we are in one of my favourite places doing one of my favourite activities, walking Bella. We are just behind Northwich tip – nice! Northwich is a mid-Cheshire town famous for salt production and the Drill Field, the former home of Northwich Victoria, which was supposedly the oldest football ground in the world. The ground is covered by houses now! Just down the road to the west of town is the village of Hartford, which is where I live and where this story begins.

The venue for the walk doesn't sound exciting, does it, but it's a lovely place to be, believe me! Feeling the warm sun on your face and seeing it light up the countryside on either side of the river you would not believe that it was January. The mud on the edges of the man-made path is a reminder of wetter days but today has more than made up for that. Bella, despite being unable to see clearly, is chasing sticks and diving headlong into the cold water. Sue keeps wondering where she's disappeared to but I know my dog. She won't be far away. It crosses my mind how important my four-legged friend has been to me over the last few dramatic years.

As Sue, Dave and I make our leisurely way round the course the orange 'RECORD' light on Dave's machine comes on and we reminisce about times past when my sisters, Jessica and Naomi, and I spent many happy hours with Sue and Dave's three girls Helen, Kathryn and Gillian. Sue and Dave had come to Hartford when Dave had been appointed head of The Grange Preparatory and Kindergarten School in the village. Sue, also a teacher, was taking time off to look after Helen and Kathryn. Gillian was soon to follow some six months after they arrived in Cheshire. Sue and Mum met up and triggered a long-lasting friendship between our two families. All six of us went to Hartford County Primary School.

The Mitchells' house in Park Lane in Hartford was about a mile or so from where we lived on Chester Road. We got to know it very well.

Sue Mitchell: I would pick the six of them up from school and a normally quiet neighbourhood would be shattered by loud shrieks as they let off steam on the short distance back to our house.

Sue would often look after all of us while Mum was at work. She made us mince and potatoes and I used to tell Mum how tasty it was, hoping that she would make it for us! Funnily enough, I had the same meal in hospital in Southport many years later and it reminded me of the Mitchells. The six of us must have been a handful for Sue at times. She would take us all to Northwich Swimming Baths on her own, quite an achievement!

Sue: On Tuesday the girls used to watch the Sooty Show *before going swimming. They all piled into the car and Hannah's mother Fran would join us at the end of the session to help dry and dress them.*

We had lots of fun and there was plenty of laughter. Sue would organise old-fashioned party games on birthdays and I used to be brilliant at sucking peas up on the end of a straw!

It's funny what you remember, isn't it? One thing that I can still picture is their stairs; they had gaps between the steps and you could peep down through them. I used to sit at the top and pretend to be a teacher. I was dead bossy and horrible! I also remember playing ambulances and using all their stock of toilet rolls for bandages!

Kathryn Mitchell: We used to get up to all sorts of games. Sumo wrestling went a bit too far. We stuffed cushions up our vests and tucked our knickers up our bottoms. I managed to knock one of Jessica's teeth out!

Helen Mitchell: Many a time we would eat my sister Gillian's sweets. Mum and Dad had bought her a miniature sweet shop as a present and it contained real sweets. We'd run upstairs to Gillian's bedroom after school and munch some!

Sue kept a jar full of packets of sweets like Skittles. I was always asking Helen if she could persuade her mum to let us have a packet.

When we were with the Mitchells I would sometimes show off to the others. Because I was the oldest of the six girls I thought I was the coolest! I was certainly mischievous. At our house I would dial a number on the telephone when Mum and Dad were not around and hang up when it was answered.

Helen: That's not all! Sometimes Hannah would make up accents and say something like, 'Hello, is that Hamish?' in a Scottish voice. Then Fran would return with bagels and Hannah would slam the phone down straight away. I bet the Roses had massive bills because Hannah did it all the time! We thought it was really funny. One reason I liked to go to Hannah's was that we could watch Saved by the Bell, *the American sitcom. Mum and Dad didn't let us watch it, but I seem to think that Dad became a fan!*

I got chicken pox once and passed it on to the other five. We had been on holiday with Grandma and Grandad and missed the ferry at St Malo. We had to drive through the night to catch another near Caen. When we finally got home I was covered in spots. Inevitably, the others also suffered and I was really miffed because when I returned to school they were all off at the same time enjoying themselves.

Sue: *Hannah caught it a couple of weeks before the others. Fran was just starting a new job and I offered to look after Hannah who was covered in spots. I had to collect the others from school so put Hannah in the push chair. She was exceptionally annoyed when she had to go back to school a couple of weeks later and the others were at our house playing in the paddling pool and having a great time.*

You are reading a deliberate attempt to paint a picture of a very happy, not far from the ordinary childhood. Beyond Helen, Kathryn and Gillian there were many other friends as well. Most were connected with Hartford County Primary School. In my year there was Rachel Hendry, Fiona Maxwell, Elizabeth Scott, Edward Belcher and Michael Jones, amongst others. My friends and I grew up together and our parents got on well so we would often see each other at parties.

Helen: *Hannah was a clever girl who always wanted to create fun and that's why she had so many friends. We were always busy at primary school. We used to get certificates for each club we were in and we got loads between us. In Gardening Club we had to regularly water plants in the courtyard which was in the centre of the school buildings. One day, Hannah got the hosepipe and somehow managed to spray water over the large windows alongside the hall! We were supposed to crush cans as well, for Recycling Club I think, and kept flicking them up in the air and doing all sorts of silly things with them.*

We were really environmentally friendly at school; there was also a conservation area, but I think it was just a massively overgrown bit of land. I enjoyed primary school, worked hard and generally stayed out of trouble, though Miss Winnington once told me off in front of the whole Year 6 class for rolling my skirt up so that it looked short! I cried my eyes out!

Helen: *Fran told Hannah off once for kissing one of the boys behind a shed at school! One playground game I remember was 'Kiss Chase'. We used to run deliberately slowly if a boy we liked was 'on', otherwise we'd run like mad to stay away! One thing* *that still makes me smile is when Hannah asked my mum what 'public hair' was! We found it in a book about growing up! Mum soon put us right on that issue: it was 'pubic hair'!*

The other day I was trying to get through Hartford for an appointment and I was thinking, *Why is all this traffic being held up when I'm in a hurry?* Then a string of floats came past and I realised that it was the annual Rose Fete. Pam was with me at the time. You'll find out more about her later! Pam didn't know about the Rose Fete and asked me what it was all about. Out spilled more memories!

Hartford school children would dress up and parade annually and help raise money for the National Society for the Prevention of Cruelty to Children. Every year we moved into a different category and every second year the girls were able to have a new dress which was made from a specific design and colour range. In the end, a few would graduate into one of the main roles in the piece. The process involved a lot of practising and pageantry and was a highlight of village life as well as raising money for a good cause.

I remember being the bouquet bearer one year and thinking, 'Mum's going to make me a lovely dress for this special occasion!' I shouldn't have raised my hopes too much. She bought one at Scope, a charity shop in Northwich! When people asked me where I'd got my dress from I'd tell them I'd had it made for me.

Fran Rose (Mum): *I should add, Hannah, that I made three dresses one year, all with a flowery design, and they are still in the dressing-up box at my school!*

Bonfire Night and Christmas were further opportunities to get together to have fun. Hartford was a really nice place to grow up in and I was fortunate to know so many lovely people.

Life was good and I was always busy. There was gym, swimming and short tennis while our friend Stuart Dornford-May put on theatre productions with us at Davenham Theatre. I loved Roald Dahl's *Fantastic Mr Fox* where I was one of the foxes. I also learned to play both the flute and piano. I've still got the flute upstairs, but we are going to get rid of our family piano. Nobody uses it, to be fair. I learnt a piece on it and I can still remember the finger positions so well that I could talk someone through it note by note.

There is many a time when I wish I could turn back the clock and be young again...

I should introduce my family properly before I go any further because you will read a lot about them through the book.

Fran, my mum, is a teacher who taught for many years at Greenbank Residential School, a school for special needs children on the Hartford campus not far from my secondary school, St Nicholas High. Mum is a very kind lady who smiles a lot and is always putting others' needs ahead of her own. We are so alike in character. By the time this book is in your hands, Mum will have taken a well-deserved retirement.

My dad, Howie, is a microbiologist who has worked in Bootle, near Liverpool, for 25 years at Mast Diagnostics. They supply products for clinical, industrial and veterinary testing around the world and have subsidiary companies in Germany and France. Dad, like Mum, is a big Manchester City supporter, and he loves gadgets and cooking. He specialises in hot, spicy dishes which have hit the back of the throat of many a guest round our table! Mum and Dad have a lot of friends and love to entertain them. I remember once when the Mitchells were with us, among others, and Dad tried some new indoor fireworks. The plan quickly backfired as smoke filled the room and everyone had to evacuate. It wasn't just the food that was hot that night!

Jessica, also known as Jess, is the middle sister and she is 27 years old. Jess did a Fashion and Textiles degree in Manchester where she now lives and works. It's handy for trips to see City! She shares my Dad's wicked sense of humour! Naomi, the youngest, is 25 and living at home at the moment, which is nice for me! Naomi went to Liverpool University after school. She combined studying for a degree in Business and Communication with an active night life (!) and now has a job as a marketing executive for a firm on the Gadbrook Industrial Estate a few miles away from home on the south side of Northwich. There we are, introductions made. Now you know who I am talking about!

Without feeling the need to rush, Sue, Dave and I make our way round the loop that has been specially created for walkers. Other dogs rush up to Bella along the way and we stop to chat with their owners. Bella 'performs', but she is some way off the path and, rather naughtily, we decide to turn our back on the deposit and move on! It is such a calm day and the combination of lovely weather and happy memories makes me feel good.

All too soon, we return to the car park. My personal assistant gets out of the car to greet us and helps me as I guide my electric wheelchair carefully up the ramp at the back of the car. I'm hoping that there isn't a lot of mud on the wheels because my dad threatens to kill me when that happens! I drive my wheelchair by pushing against a bar at the back of my head while one at each side of my head alters the direction. There's also a small screen that tells me which mode I am in. I have also got a horn and lights. I negotiate the chair on to the locking device that will keep me safe and secure during the short journey home for a cup of tea and more memories to put down on tape. I think we'll stop at the baker's shop on the way!

CHAPTER THREE
Anxious Times

'Momentarily I noticed a look of concern on her face.'

I moved on from primary school and entered my teenage years as a pupil at St Nicholas Catholic High School in Hartford. It had been a parting of the ways at age 11 because the majority of Mrs Jones's Year 6 class moved on to Hartford High School which was not too far away on the same campus. Mum and Dad liked the standard of discipline at St Nicholas and there is a Catholic strand running through the family on my mum's side. My dad was from a Jewish background in Manchester. An interesting combination!

I was a normal schoolgirl who had the same hopes and aspirations as any other teenager. I was really enjoying school life. Having been used to doing so many different activities in my early years through primary school I still participated in everything I could, whether it be netball, tennis or singing in the school choir. I wanted to be involved all the time. I loved having people around me and had developed a great group of school friends. I'm going to bring some into my story right now...

Lizzy: In our first year at high school we went on a school trip to North Wales. Hannah was in my dorm. She used to get really badly homesick and woke me up on the first night, shouting, 'Lizzy, Lizzy, I can't sleep!' At the time I had a watch with dogs on it and all I could think to say to her was: 'Look at the dogs, Hannah! Look at the dogs!' She always brings that up, even today. That trip was probably the first time our friendship really blossomed.

Karen: *Hannah was a real hit with the boys on that trip to Wales!*

Sarah: *Hannah and I were in different forms and our main contact was through choir which we really enjoyed. We went on various choir tours together and were both miserable on a German trip. She was very homesick and I was unhappy. We were complaining all the time!*

Anna: *Hannah really didn't want to go to Germany. When we arrived we were absolutely starving. We were placed with a German family and all we got was hot water with carrots in and black bread which neither of us would eat. Back in our room we feasted on my one remaining chocolate bar.*

Kate: *Hannah and I sat together in RE and kept getting told off for talking! We had a lot in common. She was studious, sporty and very funny. We would gossip about boys and the latest fashions.*

Karen: *Hannah was great at sport and I was worried if I ever had to race or play against her.*

Anna: *On non-uniform days Hannah always wore the coolest things such as sports jumpers and Kappa pull-off joggers. She would have the newest clothes at the school discos. She and Karen wore the same shoes one time, massive patent white high heels with platforms.*

Karen: *I once fell down Hannah's stairs because I was wearing her five-inch heels to go to the cinema with her!*

Kate: *There would be the usual round of birthday parties, school discos and cinema visits.*

Karen: *We had a jewellery-making party for Hannah's 12th birthday and Howie showed us videos of Hannah as a baby.*

It's funny how they have mentioned school trips which didn't go according to plan! I'm not surprised that they talked about me being homesick. I used to be dreadful! Helen has a good example to show how bad I was, from a few years earlier:

> **Helen:** I certainly do! We had a caravan and kept it on the drive at our house in Park Lane. One night, Hannah came for a sleepover in the caravan with some other friends. The planning of it was dead exciting and we were all looking forward to the adventure. Despite being only about a mile and a half from home Hannah was soon missing it! One of us got on the baby alarm which we had with us, and sent a message through to Mum and Dad inside the house! 'Hello, Susan and David, Hannah wants to go home!' Fran and Howie had to come and pick her up! I remember thinking it was really late, like about three o'clock, but it was probably only about half past ten.

Oh Helen, I feel so embarrassed looking back at that! At the time I blamed some sausages I'd eaten for making me feel sick but I'm pretty sure that was an excuse! What a wimp!

> **Helen:** And while I'm on the subject, how about Guide camp at Pettypool Wood? Once again, Hannah was homesick and the camp was only about two miles from her home!

My friends and I were always together:

> **Anna:** Sleepovers became a regular feature and I remember stopping at Hannah's in the attic and telling each other ghost stories.

> **Karen:** There was a sleepover night when we all got upset and wrote notes saying what we loved about each other and spent the night crying!

Like any bunch of adolescent girls we would gossip endlessly about silly teenage things like who was the nicest boy in school or who was most popular person in the year. We discussed bands, clothes and make-up, the latest storylines on the soaps and we were obsessed with celebrities. I had a particular passion for Robbie Williams from the band Take That!

I got tickets to see Robbie Williams at the MEN to celebrate my 15th birthday. My friends and I thought we were dead grown up because we could be dropped off and left at the arena! It was the first big concert we had gone to by ourselves. We got dressed up to the nines and packed into the family Volvo. Everyone wanted the boot seats which faced back down the road. You're supposed to be about age seven to be in those! Just to make the night even better, Mum stopped at McDonald's on the way.

It happened to be on a school night and I had begged Mum to let us sleep at our house after. When we got back we had to do our maths homework until two or three in the morning. We got a bit stroppy with each other because of the late hour and eventually crashed out on the lounge floor. We were also a bit snappy with each other in school the following day because we were so tired but it had been a brilliant concert and one which proved to be very poignant as my story unfolded.

Robbie sent me a get well card after I became ill, but I was frustrated that I never managed to meet him. I tried, believe me I tried! The Make-A-Wish Foundation nearly made it happen. It was established in the UK in 1986 and, since then, has granted over 8300 wishes to children and young people fighting life-threatening conditions. I got involved and my first choice was to meet Robbie. My second was to meet Ant and Dec. Neither happened in the end. I left my hospital bed and, once again, joined my friends to see Robbie in concert at the Manchester Evening News Arena. The day started with a make-over at the Trafford Centre, then we had a box for the night. We tried to get a message through to Robbie right up to the final minutes before he went on stage but it didn't happen. My wish didn't come true that night. Rosanne was one of my friends who went with me.

Rosanne: *It was a really emotional night when we went to see Robbie because we all loved him. We hung around waiting and hoping, but a meeting didn't happen.*

As we sang along to the songs we had played countless times thoughts inevitably turned back to the 15th birthday concert. It had been in the March before I became ill in the May. A month later we had all been on a school trip to Belgium and throughout the trip we were listening to Robbie's new album, *I've Been Expecting You*, and, in particular, the song *Strong*. The Make-A-Wish concert brought it all back. We heard the songs once again and they revived memories of carefree days. My friends still say they can't hear songs like *Angels* without thinking of me and my illness.

St Nicholas was such an important part of my life. Don't let me make you think that all I wanted to do was gossip and eye up the lads. In the classroom I was determined to make a good impression on my teachers and friends and spent far too much of my time worrying about getting things exactly right, something that I have done throughout my life. I have always been, and will always be, a worrier and during my high school years it was important that I had everything I needed for school each day, got good grades and was well-liked.

Anna: Hannah and I would always ring each other the night before homework was due in and worry about the fact that we hadn't done it, when really we should just have got on with it!

I have realised more and more, looking back from an adult perspective, how much I loved school. Everything that has happened since adds more poignancy to that feeling and it makes me really sad that I did not get to develop my teenage years along with everybody else and in the way I had dreamed.

Anyway, that's the background filled in. I think it's about time you heard what happened to turn my life upside down. I became ill in 1999, a couple of months after my 15th birthday. Life was never the same again.

It all started during the second week of May and top priority for me at the time was a school water sports trip to France. Despite my poor track record when spending time away from home, I was really looking forward to this one. I was also busy revising for examinations, desperate to get the results that I wanted and deserved. The French trip was not only a great chance to take a break from my studies but also to enjoy some quality time with my friends away from our parents!

The first sign of trouble, though I wasn't to realise the implications at the time, was a pain which started to develop in my shoulder and across the top of my back. It wasn't that bad at first and I just thought it was a pulled muscle from playing netball so I carried on going to school.

I'd bought a new swimsuit for the trip to France and was trying it on at Grandma Frances's house when I started to get the pain further across my back. At first it was just a dull ache, then it became more noticeable. I carried on going to school because I didn't want to miss any end-of-year exams, but the pain showed no signs of going away. In fact, it got steadily worse as the days passed and to the stage where it was really uncomfortable and hard to bear. Strange feelings started to develop in my legs. One leg felt hot, the other cold. Very odd. There were a number of possible reasons for the pains in my back and shoulders, but once those contrasting feelings began in my legs I was into new territory and became increasingly worried.

One of my friends was to admit much later, 'I always remember when you were first having your back pain at school. I knew how well you wanted to do in your exams and told you that I thought the backache was caused by bending over desks too much and working too hard!' She always feels really guilty about that!

Anna: The day before Hannah went into hospital I remember her complaining of a bad back and working out how she would get a lift home as she had to walk home that day. I suggested to her that it was probably period pains.

Fran: I had arranged to go to see Oh What a Night at the theatre with my school. I asked Martin, our school caretaker, if he would pick Hannah and Jessica up and drop them off at home because I wouldn't be there at the normal time. I remember saying to Martin that Hannah had a painful back, but I wasn't going to be home until about six o'clock. Martin did as I had asked and when Howie and I got back Hannah seemed a bit perkier, so much so that we decided to go to see Manchester City play Wigan Athletic in the Division Two play-offs as we had tickets. We left Hannah in charge. We had been driving for about ten minutes and had got as far as the Horns Inn on the A49, for those of you who know the area, when we got a phone call from Jessica to say, 'I think you should come home because Hannah's crying.' Her back was hurting even more so we abandoned our plans for the match and turned round.

Jessica Rose: *Hannah had been complaining about her back, but at the time we thought she was just saying it because of exams and stuff. Now, for the first time, Naomi and I thought that there might be more to it. She was really in a lot of pain.*

Fran: *We decided that enough was enough and that Hannah should go to the doctor's the next morning. We genuinely thought that she might have hurt her back by overdoing it. I stayed up with Hannah all night and she kept talking about one leg being hot and one being cold. The pain was making her feel sick but, despite that, she was still insistent on going into school the next day.*

Mum made the appointment in the morning as the pain was threatening to overtake my whole body.

Fran: *I got dressed, rang school and told them that I would be a bit late... I walked back into school 15 months later! I hated being off and was really sorry, but by the time I made my long-overdue return, I didn't need to do any explaining!*

I remember being upstairs in my bedroom getting dressed to go. I wanted to make sure that I looked as good for the doctor as I would for Robbie Williams! It mattered to me, even for a GP appointment. Any 15-year-old girl reading this would understand where I was coming from.

I pulled my jeans out of the wardrobe and my GAP hoodie. I did my hair for the umpteenth time and took one last look in the mirror before heading back downstairs. Little was I to know, but that would be the last time that I would be able to walk down a flight of stairs. I have never seen that bedroom again. I came down, out through the front door and into the car. I left the house able-bodied for the very last time. There were no tears shed, there was no consideration of the implications because I was fully expecting that the pain would lift and that life would return to normal.

So, on the morning of Thursday, 19 May, we drove straight to Danebridge Medical Centre in Northwich for our appointment with the doctor. She was lovely and gave me a good checking over. She tested my reflexes by tapping my leg with a hammer. There was no response. Momentarily, I noticed a look of concern on her face. I've always been very good at picking up signs like that. I just knew that it was something serious. She got me to explain how I felt. Mum told me that I described it well. The doctor then set the alarm bells ringing when she said that we needed to get this checked out. The slightest thing sets me off in a worry so you can imagine how I took this news! She gave us a letter to take to the Countess of Chester Hospital and offered to arrange for an ambulance to get us there, but Mum said that she would drive us the 16-mile journey.

I was in severe pain by now. It was a very hot day, the sort that I normally love, but I was in no mood to enjoy the sunshine as Mum and I were stuck in a traffic jam for what seemed like forever. This only served to make the pain appear even worse.

When I got out of the car at the hospital I was really struggling to walk so had to lean on Mum. It was a real effort to get from the car to reception. We were put in a nice room where two doctors began a further investigation. They asked all sorts of questions like, 'Have you had a sports injury?' 'Have you pulled your back?'

It was about four o'clock when another medic met us and started a further examination. He requested an MRI scan immediately. Most people will know of this by the three initials, but the full scientific term is Magnetic Resonance Imaging. It is a type of scan that is used to diagnose health conditions that affect organs, tissue and bone. An MRI scanner uses strong magnetic fields and radio waves to produce detailed images of the inside of the body. It looks like a large tube and you lie inside it during the scan. By the time you've finished reading this book you'll have enough information to do a Science A-level!

Anxiety levels rose even further when the doctor was told that there wasn't enough time to perform an MRI scan that day as they tended not to do them after five o'clock. Thankfully, he insisted and got his way. It happened and, at last, we had an explanation. An attack on my spinal cord had caused a large amount of swelling and this was what was causing the pain. He told us that he had only seen two cases of this in his career and that it was a condition known as transverse myelitis.

If you don't like or understand long medical explanations then skip the next couple of paragraphs, but I recommend you stick with it – you might learn something! The following description comes from a fact sheet produced by the National Institute of Neurological Disorders and Stroke:

Transverse myelitis is a neurological disorder caused by inflammation across both sides of one level, or segment, of the spinal cord. The term *myelitis* refers to inflammation of the spinal cord; *transverse* simply describes the position of the inflammation, that is, across the width of the spinal cord. Attacks of inflammation can damage or destroy myelin, the fatty insulating substance that covers nerve cell fibres. This damage causes nervous system scars that interrupt communications between the nerves in the spinal cord and the rest of the body.

Symptoms of transverse myelitis include a loss of spinal cord function over several hours to several weeks. What usually begins as a sudden onset of lower back pain, muscle weakness, or abnormal sensations in the toes and feet can rapidly progress to more severe symptoms, including paralysis, urinary retention, and loss of bowel control. Although some patients recover from transverse myelitis with minor or no residual problems, others suffer permanent impairments that affect their ability to perform ordinary tasks of daily living.

Anyway, medical lecture over! I did not have all that information handed to me on a laminated card at the time. All I did know was that I was in great pain and worrying about what it all meant. We were told that I needed to go to a hospital with an intensive care unit and that they were admitting me to Alder Hey Children's Healthcare Hospital in Liverpool to see a neurologist. Naomi and Jess arrived with Dad, and Mum looked really upset as she told them such awful news.

The doctor who had arranged the MRI scan suggested that I might come back to the Countess for rehabilitation and I asked, stupidly when I think back, 'Can my friends come for a sleepover?'! I thought that there would be rooms big enough for that to happen and it showed how my mind worked!

Fran: *It felt surreal because Hannah was chatting normally and asking if she could still go on her French trip. She ate a ham sandwich and a blackcurrant yogurt and was watching* Home and Away! *In many respects she seemed typically well. There didn't seem to be any reason why she needed to go to intensive care.*

Naomi Rose: *I clearly remember Hannah being at the Countess of Chester. Dad picked us up from school. Jess was at rounders and really annoyed because she had to leave early! Dad said that Hannah had gone into hospital. We couldn't find a parking space at Chester so had to park a long way away. Finally, we got to Mum who was really, really upset. Then we went to see Hannah. There were* Friends *pictures on the hospital walls which I thought was really cool! When I got to the room I saw Hannah trying to walk to the toilet, but she was struggling because her leg was dragging.*

At half past eight, some 12 hours after Mum had rung for an appointment in Northwich, an ambulance was ready to take me to Liverpool. I chatted to two lovely female paramedics whose job was clearly to distract me from my physical pain and mental anguish on the 21-mile journey between the two hospitals. Something was seriously wrong as the pain in my back was unbearable and I was beginning to lose more feeling in both my legs.

CHAPTER FOUR
The Illness Takes Hold

'Will I be able to go to France?'

Alder Hey is one of Europe's biggest and busiest children's hospitals. Founded in 1914, it was originally intended as a workhouse for sick paupers. Now, it provides care for over 200,000 children and young people each year.

When I arrived I was put in my own room on Ward D3. I was so relieved to be in my own space. A registrar saw me first, then the neurologist came to chat to Mum, Dad and me about what to expect. He told us that the illness was going to get worse before it got better but that I should only be in the hospital for a few weeks. All I could think about was how much I wanted to go on the school trip to France as I had been so excited about it. I must have driven the doctor mad with an endless string of questions during that first night: 'When will I be out?' 'Will I be able to go to France?'

Fran: Alder Hey seemed so unfamiliar on arrival but little was I to know how well we were going to get to know the miles of long corridors that criss-crossed the building.

Jessica: We followed Hannah to Alder Hey. There was a picture of Mowgli, the child from The Jungle Book, *on the wall. I remember thinking that Hannah was probably a bit old for that now. The murals on the wall brought home that Alder Hey was a children's hospital. Hannah was at the top end of the age range and not a child any more. Any older and she would probably have gone into a normal hospital.*

Fran: *Actually, Jess, Alder Hey took up to age 18 and occasionally there were older children than Hannah.*

Writing the book has, apart from many other things, shown me how much I have forgotten about life in Alder Hey over the coming weeks and months. I have learned so much from listening to Mum, Dad, Jess and Naomi. Their recollections for this book have filled a lot of gaps in a memory dimmed by pain and medication. It has been an important outcome for me.

Fran: *By the next day, Friday, 20 May, Hannah was losing more sensation. Amidst all this gloom and worry, however, there were reminders that life still had to go on. There were other things to consider including Jess's need to get to a Boyzone concert in Manchester. I drove her and also stopped by at Howie's mum and dad's house while I was over there.*

Jessica: *The Boyzone concert was a couple of days after Hannah became ill and it was really good of Mum to take me and my friends as well as bringing us home. Looking back I can't believe that she did it or that I let her do it at that crucial time. When she brought us back to Hartford she drove into the wrong drive by mistake, a couple of doors down. I was so embarrassed in front of my friends! I suppose, looking back, I can't blame Mum too much.*

Fran: *From the Saturday onwards Hannah knew little of what was happening due to sedation. She was getting quite panicky and concern was increasing over her breathing. Sue and Dave came on the Saturday and while they were there the neurologist took Howie and me into a separate room and said that things were very bad. We were to prepare for the worst scenario. The situation was devastatingly awful.*

Chris Mather (friend): *I had been at Fran's during the week when Hannah was clearly not well. It looked like she would need to be seen by a doctor. Two or three days later Fran had taken*

Hannah and she rang me from the hospital on the night Hannah was admitted to say that she was critically ill and that she was having the last rites. I couldn't understand how it had escalated to such a degree.

Grandma and Grandpa visited. Sue brought me some shower gel with glitter in and a roller ball. It's funny that I remember things like that so clearly when much has been dimmed by time. As we looked back while writing the book together, Sue and Dave told me how scared I became when Dad said that he was going to have to stay overnight with me. He slept nearby on a camp bed. I was to be 'specialled', which meant that there was a nurse allocated just to me. I was then given morphine, a drug used to treat acute and chronic severe pain, and it was about this time that they started to talk about taking me to intensive care.

Over the next 48 hours normal feelings began to disappear. Movement started to drain away in my legs and then upward through my body. I noticed this particularly in my hands because I was finding it hard to grip. I tried to open a packet of crisps, but I couldn't hold the packet tightly enough and failed miserably. I had difficulty going to the toilet as my walking had become increasingly unstable. The doctor then came and explained to me that I was going to have a catheter fitted as I had not been to the toilet for a while. This is a tube which allows the hospital to remove urine from my bladder. Mum couldn't be there with me when it was fitted. I was scared and embarrassed. I was also very self-conscious about the doctors seeing my body. It wasn't an easy experience for a 15-year-old girl.

I can remember desperately wanting to speak to my friends so Dad pushed me in a wheelchair to the nearest pay phone where I could call Rosanne to say 'Hi!' When I called her house her dad told me that all my friends were actually on their way to the hospital to visit me but it was meant to be a surprise so I would have to act that way when they came! It felt so good to see them. I don't remember much about the conversation we had, but I do remember still having some mobility at that stage.

Lizzy: *Fran told us that Hannah had lost some movement, but we had no idea what was to come. I've lost count of the times that Fran has said, 'You're so good for coming!' and we would always reply that we did it because, first and foremost, Hannah is our friend. Obviously she was ill and that was a trigger for why we were there but for us at the time we just thought: 'Let's go and see Hannah.'*

The girls had been on a trip as part of their work towards the Duke of Edinburgh's Award and they brought me a sunflower toy which could be hung up by my bed.

Lizzy: *Yes, Rosanne, Anna, Kate, Susan and I went on an expedition and we bought Hannah this kind of hanging flower with legs on.*

Susan: *We had done mock exams on the Friday and the rest of us went on D of E over the weekend. It was my birthday on the Sunday. Ours was a close group. I didn't start at St Nicholas until Year 8 but Hannah and I both had younger sisters and this brought us closer together. We had quite a bit in common and bonded over many chats about how annoying they could be!*

Rosanne: *I will always remember the day Hannah went into hospital because it was my mum's birthday. Some of the timings of visits remain hazy but I clearly remember visiting her in hospital before she had lost all her mobility. She was trying to use her inhaler but couldn't hold it to make it work.*

I have always been blessed by having the company of close and loyal friends and this was a time when I needed them more than ever. They didn't let me down, reacting immediately to the news that I was in hospital.

I cannot remember the following days too well but, apparently, I went for a second MRI scan and Dad was told that it showed lots of inflammation. My nurse was constantly observing and noting my progress. The pain continued to be awful and the neurologist conceded that the aggressive speed of the virus was baffling. He was wondering if it really was transverse myelitis.

Fran: Tuesday was an awful day. It was still less than a week since we had gone to the doctor's but Hannah had little feeling left in her arms and hands.

I had to have a lumbar puncture to collect some fluid for analysis. To help combat the pain, the nurse tried to get me into 'a different place' where I could feel some pleasurable, positive thoughts. She asked me where my favourite place in the world was and I said the Trafford Centre – a large indoor shopping centre in Greater Manchester! I felt so stupid once I'd given that answer, but she went along with me and tried to get me to imagine going in and out of all my favourite shops.

Fran: Trust you, Hannah! Out of all the places round the world to choose from...!

Well, you know how much I liked shopping, Mum!

Fran: Nothing's changed there, Hannah!

The next picture I have in my mind is of lying in my hospital bed with my dad still on the camp bed on the floor next to me. I asked him if I was going to lose all the feeling in my arms as well as my legs and he reassured me that it wasn't going to happen. That's what he had to say to keep my spirits up but whether he totally believed it was another matter. Due to his scientific background, Dad was to have more than a layman's understanding as my story unfolded and this was to prove beneficial on a number of occasions. However, there are also times when too much knowledge can be a dangerous thing.

A nurse came to see me. She was looking at the possibility that my breathing might deteriorate. She said to me that if the swelling on my spinal cord became any worse, I would possibly have to rely on a ventilator and be moved to the intensive care unit. She attached me to a monitor designed to record my oxygen levels and heart rate. It all seemed so dramatic at the time, to be hooked up to machines and monitors. It was something that I had previously only seen in the popular BBC hospital series *Casualty* on television! Although I had become aware that something had taken control of my body I was still pretty much in the dark as to the extent of the damage that had been done and the implications.

Day by day I was losing the ability to perform normal everyday tasks and panicking more and more about just how long this deterioration would last. So much had happened in less than a week as my body was being invaded by unwelcome pain. What would I be left with when it all died down? Was it to be a temporary setback or permanent paralysis?

CHAPTER FIVE

Intensive Care

'I felt so ill that I simply couldn't understand what was going on.'

The pain just would not go away and morphine continued to be prescribed for me. The much-discussed move to the intensive care unit finally took place on the Wednesday after I arrived at Alder Hey. This was the place where the most serious illnesses and injuries were treated. It was staffed by highly trained doctors and critical care nurses and inhabited by patients who needed constant monitoring. It was an unforgiving environment.

> **Fran:** *The intensive care unit at Alder Hey was half made up of critically ill children and young people like Hannah and the other half was children who had had cardiac surgery, particularly newborn babies.*

I was sedated for a number of days, but my ever-present mum and dad stayed nearby. I'll let Mum take over for the next bit because, to be honest, I didn't remember very much about this period!

> **Fran:** *Well, we were really scared that the sedation meant that we would never be able to speak to Hannah again. At least she was not now in pain. When Hannah went to intensive care she immediately became a ventilated patient. Dr Andrew Selby, the consultant in charge of the ventilation, took control from the neurologist. The treatment of disorders connected with Hannah's nervous system became less of a factor after that and*

her breathing and respiratory problems took over as the main cause for concern.

That changed the whole outlook. They didn't ignore the neurology [nervous system] but they admitted that the complications triggered by the neurology became the bigger issue. Hannah went to Alder Hey because they had an intensive care unit and the specialists felt all along that it was inevitable that she would finish up in that unit. Once she had been admitted to the hospital, they realised that she would need ventilation and that became the major factor.

I must admit that I wasn't aware of all that at the time. I saw the ventilation as a temporary thing that would get Hannah through a crisis. I failed to see that it would become a permanent issue. After what the neurologist had said about things getting worse before they got better it appeared that Hannah had a 12-week window for things to improve.

When I woke up a few days later I was unable to speak but did not know why. The reason was that I had had a tracheotomy. In this procedure a doctor placed a tube into my windpipe to aid breathing. I was now dependent on a ventilator. It was to become a constant companion and mechanically allowed me to move air into and out of my lungs. I also had regular measurements taken for the oxygen in my blood and my heart rate.

The whole thing seemed surreal. I can just remember being unable to hold my head up and feeling very weak. I know it sounds strange but it didn't even occur to me that I was unable to move my body. I felt so ill that I simply couldn't understand what was going on.

Fran: *When the sedation was lifted and Hannah responded it was a huge relief. We knew that she was still with us.*

When I moved up to intensive care a doctor had already spoken to Mum and Dad about the option of staying on the hospital grounds. Alder Hey provided an amazing facility for families. It was called Ronald McDonald House. Ronald McDonald Houses are run by an independent charity and located in or near to hospitals, so that families can be close to their seriously ill children at any time of the day or night. They are open all year round and provide not only free accommodation, but also a place for families to rest, relax, cook, clean, wash clothing and be together away from the stress of the hospital ward. Where possible, every bedroom has a telephone directly linked to the hospital ward. Knowing they can have direct contact with the ward should an emergency arise at any time of the day or night gives families peace of mind and helps them to relax.

Ronald McDonald House at Alder Hey Hospital, Liverpool, is the largest in Europe. Since opening in 1993 with just 26 bedrooms, the House has expanded twice and now offers accommodation to 84 families each night. The House has accommodated over 16,000 families in its 20-year history. There are now 69 family bedrooms and 15 family apartments for long-stay families, who need to stay for six months or more. For the Rose family, it provided the most wonderful base which allowed us to be together during my time in Alder Hey and my mum and dad appreciated it so much that they have regularly helped raise funds through a variety of events. As my dad already worked in the Liverpool area it made sense for him to spend most nights here and it was so reassuring for me to know that my parents were close by.

Fran: Howie and I shared duties at Ronald McDonald House. To be fair, it was easier for him to go to work the next day from there and with me at home I could get the girls to school more easily.

Ronald McDonald House provided a smaller room initially but then a larger family room which meant that at weekends and school holidays Mum, Dad, Jessica and Naomi could stay at the hospital, as my time at Alder Hey was clearly developing into a long haul.

Howie Rose (Dad): I always remember a sign on the wall of our room in Ronald McDonald House: 'This room costs £14 per day.' It stuck with me and since then we've been trying to pay back that £14 for each day we have used the facility. We organise a kind of garden party every year and RMH is a nominated charity at my Rotary Club where we've raised about £1000 each Christmas for the last three years.

I think that Jess was at the hospital with Mum and Dad during the early days but Naomi was staying with our grandparents as Mum and Dad thought that it would be too distressing for her to be around the hospital. Jess was 13 at the time and Naomi only 11. They got some time off school, I seem to remember.

Naomi: *Hannah's right. I went to Grandma and Grandpa's when she first went in. I had bagels every day! They also took me to places like Roma's, which was an Italian café, and the Arndale Centre in Manchester. They tried really hard to keep me occupied and bought me a few things. I remember them bringing me to see Hannah. They took me on the train. They warned me, 'You might not want to go in.' Intensive care was quite scary. Hannah was lying on the bed. The room was in darkness apart from a circle of light around her.*

I also went to Sue and Dave's to stay and we went to the Blackpool Pleasure Beach. Hannah was so jealous when she found out! [I certainly was!] *I definitely missed some school time but it was after the SAT exams I think. I do remember going to North Wales on the end-of-year school trip. It was just after Hannah had been admitted and I remember how nice everyone was to me.*

A lot of the time was spent between the ward and Ronald McDonald House but, for a change of scenery, Mum would take Jess and me to the shops nearby and we would go to ASDA, KFC and McDonald's regularly. I remember the hospital shop. It sold Ribena and cans were just 25p each! I'd get money from Mum and Dad to get things which I'd take back to Ronald McDonald House. One day Jess and I wanted a ploughman's lunch from the hospital restaurant. Mum brought it to our room in Ronald McDonald House and we were in our pyjamas on a kind of camping mattress watching the Tweenies! *Shortly after, there was a knock on the door. We couldn't bring ourselves to answer because we weren't allowed to eat in the room and because we didn't want to admit we were watching the* Tweenies *at our age!*

On another day, I remember we were all getting to sleep when I looked around and saw this thing moving across my face. It was the biggest spider I had ever seen in my life. I jumped up and Dad saw it. He jumped on to the bed! The fire alarm used to go off all the time as people burnt toast.

Kathryn: *I remember going into Ronald McDonald House with Jessica and Naomi. I'm always supporting the charity, every time I go to McDonald's which is quite a lot!*

It was hard for Naomi and Jess. School holidays must have been particularly difficult because they had to spend more time in the hospital.

Although I was the focus of attention, normal life attempted to continue around me. Ronald McDonald House had a washing machine which apparently was really helpful.

Fran: *My first visit back home was nine days after Hannah had been admitted to Alder Hey. There were 24 messages on the telephone answer machine and loads of cards from well-wishers. There were some beautiful thoughts and prayers which really touched me.*

Having missed the League Two play-off semi-final between his beloved City and Wigan Athletic, Dad was keen to ensure that he kept tabs on the Wembley final against Gillingham:

Howie: *I listened to some of the match on the way to visit Hannah in hospital and managed to catch the last part on my portable radio with my earphones in and my head sticking precariously out of the window to get a better reception! I remained in that position for about half an hour. I nearly fell out with the excitement as Paul Dickov took the game into added time with a very late equaliser before goalkeeper Nicky Weaver was the hero in the penalty shoot-out.*

Manchester City in League Two! It's hard to believe that, as I write, they are the Premier League champions. Following the fortunes of the Sky Blues has been something that, as a family, we have been able to do together and we look forward to our visits to the Etihad Stadium. We have season tickets and rarely miss a match. Naomi is not as keen as the rest of us but we have shared some fantastic moments at the football, particularly in 2012 when the Sky Blues won the league for the first time and the top division title for the first time in 44 years. One of my favourite parts of match day is looking for celebrities who I can have my picture taken with! I have gathered quite a collection over the years and there's always a famous face to see at City.

Lizzy: Any opportunity to have a photograph alongside a famous person and Hannah is there!

It was hard to sense any structure in the following weeks. My mum and dad trained up in tracheotomy care while I experienced a level of pain that I had never felt before. I was still unable to speak and Mum and Dad were also given directions on how to lip read so that they could communicate with me. I began to rely on a system of clicking noises to gain people's attention!

I was not absorbing food so it was decided that I should be given a nasogastric tube in order to give me a proper, reliable drip feed and so I could receive medication. This was one of the most uncomfortable things ever. The tube was run through my nose, past my throat and down into my stomach. I clearly felt the cold sensation of the liquid passing through my nose and trickling into my throat.

Fran: Hannah would regularly have sudden bouts of anxiety. On a number of occasions I would be elsewhere and suddenly get a call to her bedside to calm her. She cried a huge amount and on one occasion she even thought she was under the bed! She was really frightened at times and I never knew what was going to greet me next when I went into her room.

The illness seemed to have had a go at all parts of my body. Another result was that my lung had collapsed and I needed regular physiotherapy. The physiotherapist would come into my room to work on my chest. This involved the nurse squirting

20 millilitres of saline down my tracheotomy into my chest and my chest being shaken to loosen any secretion. I would have a suction tube placed down my throat to remove the fluid from my lungs. I hated it. It was so uncomfortable and I remember the feeling of dread every time I knew that they were coming. The nurses were so nice, though, and we gradually became really good friends as I would see them twice a day, every day, and have a chance to build a relationship.

My friends continually amazed me throughout my whole stay in hospital. Susan's dad is a doctor so Mum and Dad felt that he could explain to her what to expect when she came to see me. I can remember one of Susan's visits really well although I was still very poorly. I had a raging temperature and this was making me hallucinate. I felt as if I had cotton wool in my hand and that I was swinging in a hammock! Crazy, man! I think that the whole experience must have been very shocking for Susan as I definitely was not myself and was too poorly to even have a conversation with her.

Susan: *Yes, it was hard to witness. I went into Alder Hey with my dad. He took me into the room and it was quite scary. In fact, it was really upsetting. Hannah was talking but not making sense and wired up to all sorts of machines. She didn't seem like Hannah at all. She had lost use of her arms and legs. To see such deterioration over a short period of time was startling.*

Celia (friend and Susan's sister): *I clearly remember when it all happened. Susan came home and was really upset. She kept asking for our dad's medical advice about what it would mean for Hannah. I could tell even at my young age that it really shook Susan.*

Rosanne: *It was a pretty rapid deterioration. Nobody really knew what was happening. I remember coming home quite shocked. Visits were really hard to begin with. In fact, my parents weren't sure that I should keep going when they saw the effect they were having on me. Hannah was really drugged up in the early days when in intensive care.*

Strangely, during visits, we could communicate with each other without any problems, even though I could not talk. It must have been all the practice that we had had while whispering and sending signals to each other during lessons! I was very lucky whilst I was in hospital as there were always visitors to keep me company. I valued every one of them for making the effort to come and see me.

My family was brilliant, my aunties and uncles and cousins were always there to see me and my grandparents were fantastic. My cousins, David and Emma, made a funny video of them singing *My Heart Will Go On* by Celine Dion.

They all used to just sit next to my bed and try to talk to me and I loved them coming. My grandparents used to bring me Beanie Babies every week. These were animals stuffed with plastic pellets which gave a flexible feel. They began to emerge as popular collectibles in the mid-1990s and became a hot toy! I think that Grandpa Lou saw it as a challenge to find me the most unusual one that he could.

Lizzy: Hannah's room started to resemble a shop, there was so much in it! I particularly remember the Beanie Babies that she had. They were cool!

I felt particularly sad when my friends reported back on the water sports holiday to France. I was still heartbroken that I could not go and I think that this must have been the first time that I realised that things were going to be different from now on. I asked about the holiday and they seemed reluctant to talk about it, probably because they felt so awful that I had missed out. In a way I didn't want to know about it because I was so jealous that I had not been able to go away with them.

The visits were important to me and to Mum and Dad because they showed that people were thinking about us and they broke the monotony of life on intensive care. Young and old alike were welcomed. The priest came, as did the head of Mum's school, and the head of St Nicholas, who came in his shorts! A pass was needed to get in and people were often kept waiting if there was something that needed to be done by the doctors or nurses. There were lots of issues around a visit.

Jessica: Hannah was obviously severely disabled but as long as she was in a hospital there was always the potential for things to get better. Whereas it was difficult to see her getting back to the way she was, I still had hope at that point. She just might get better. An abiding feeling for me was that after a couple of weeks or so Hannah was no longer ill. It was just a case of dealing with the situation we had been presented with and assessing the long-term effects of the position that she was in.

As time passed the whole situation still didn't become real and graphic to me. I had a lovely consultant who I felt totally confident with and trusted completely and this was a massive help. The doctors decided to remove my nasogastric tube and replace it with a gastrostomy tube. This was a tube that was inserted directly into my stomach as I still could not eat and swallow medication. I remember having the procedure done and wanting to show my friends when they came to visit me, not realising how horrible it was to look at. It had just been done and there was still blood around the site. I cannot believe that I made my friends look at such a disgusting thing. Mum would say, 'I am sure they don't want to see that, Hannah!' but I was convinced that they would! I soon realised that Mum was right as each of them seemed to turn a pale green colour as they looked!

A couple of months after my admission to Alder Hey, a consultant came to see me from Southport Spinal Unit. It might seem strange that I hadn't been in Southport in the first place but there were no beds available there. I would have had the benefit of specialist knowledge but, against that, they did not have a wonderful facility to match Ronald McDonald House.

Mum and Dad waited anxiously for news as the consultant examined me.

Fran: For the first 12 weeks that had been identified as the window before improvements might start we were very positive because we thought we needed that period to let things take their course. We kind of clung on to what the neurologist had said – 'it will get worse before it gets better.' These words had been used when Hannah was admitted but at least twice in our time there he took us aside and told us to expect the worst – and I mean the worst.

There's no doubt that Hannah was a mystery to both the medics and us. She was left with the damage – that's all you could say. By the end of the 12 weeks things hadn't improved so the period was kind of extended. Intensive care was a very, very difficult place when you were all under such massive pressure. I am sure that Hannah would not have realised that a lot of the time because of the medication.

We hoped that the consultant from Southport would give us some idea of what had actually happened inside my body and a clearer picture of what the future might hold. It might sound strange to you, but I had not taken in the significance of the fact that I couldn't move. I had repeatedly blocked it out of my thought processes and my emotions were constantly affected by the regular doses of medication and the constant work on my body by the doctors, nurses and physiotherapists.

The consultant greeted me and started touching my hand. He asked questions about how much feeling and movement I had. Dad came out with all his usual scientific questions. The consultant carefully explained to us that if I had not regained any feeling or movement within the first two months of injury then it would be unlikely to return again. For the first time my family was facing up to the stark reality that one of the five Roses was going to be paralysed for the rest of her life. The swelling on my spinal cord had left me with no movement from my neck down and dependent on ventilation.

I asked no questions. I shed no tears. I simply smiled and thanked him for visiting before going back to watching television. The human mind is a fascinating subject and, for reasons best known to itself, mine was refusing to acknowledge and absorb the life-changing news coming from the specialist. I was in denial. I honestly believe that the full enormity of my situation only hit me after I left Alder Hey.

I didn't even notice my parents' reaction at that time. I was in a world of my own.

Fran: I certainly didn't take it on board that life was going to become so difficult for Hannah. That realisation dawned on me when she came home from hospital for the first brief time. That was a significant moment.

My friends came to visit that day and I sat down with them and said, almost flippantly, 'A consultant came today from the spinal injuries unit and told me that I'm unlikely to walk again.' I think that I even smiled when I said it! God, what must my friends have been thinking at the time? They must've thought I was mad! Hurt and anger would have been understandable. I just smiled sweetly!

I still wasn't able to eat and drink normally but, bit by bit, I tried. Mum mashed watermelon so that I could swallow it and then I started to manage solid food. I will never forget the day when I tried to eat pizza. Oh my goodness! It was one of the worst decisions that I have ever made! The food was really dry. I remember feeling a choking sensation and then everything went black. Apparently, the pizza had stopped my breathing. The takeaway had taken it away! I needed resuscitation and fast! I can't remember the experience that well, but my parents have assured me that this was definitely not a good time.

Howie: It certainly wasn't. I got a phone call at work from the sister who asked me to get over to Alder Hey as Hannah wasn't very well. It was one of those occasions when a person does not want to look you in the eye. Paul, the physio, was crying. Hannah's heart stopped and she momentarily left us.

Thanks for mentioning Paul, Dad! Paul was so lovely to me and a bit of a celebrity, too! Did you know that he was on *Ready Steady Cook* once? I was so impressed! *Ready Steady Cook* was a cookery game show that ran on the BBC from 1994 to 2010. Members of the public had to provide chefs with a bag of ingredients bought to a limited budget, usually of £5. The two teams were symbolised by a red tomato and a green pepper on their aprons. I don't need to explain all this – I bet you used to watch it – go on, admit it!

Well, Paul asked me to pick the items that were going to be in his bag for the programme. How good is that? I made some choices and off he went for the filming. The host at the time was Fern Britton. She asked Paul the usual type of questions at the start and he told her, 'I am a physiotherapist at Alder Hey Hospital in Liverpool where I'm looking after a girl called Hannah'!

Fern said, 'Do you want to give Hannah a wave?' Paul gave me a wave and told Fern that I had picked his food. Then he lost! The next day I went to hydrotherapy and he came into the room with his green pepper apron on! That sort of thing has always impressed me.

Fran: Still on my favourite topic of food: on a positive note, I returned one evening to discover that Hannah wanted a chocolate-chip cookie! She ate it and enjoyed it! That everyday act meant a huge amount.

The amount of constant medication was triggering all kinds of side-effects throughout my body. My hair had started to thin and this was obviously a concern for a teenage girl. A doctor walked in one day and, without thinking, said, 'All your hair is falling out, Hannah!' I was absolutely devastated by this comment and Mum was really angry at the doctor for saying something so heartless. My appearance has always been important to me and my local hairdresser had offered to come to the hospital to do my hair every few weeks. Mo was a friend of the family who lived near us on Chester Road. As well as the regular visits, she popped in to blow dry my hair on my birthday.

How I look is still as important to me today as it was before I became ill, but keeping control over such a basic female need has proved difficult. I remember one day when Mum was trying to do my hair and I just burst into tears through sheer frustration. I was desperate for a mirror, a brush and two 'working' hands so that I could tackle it just as I wanted it done. It is one thing not being able to walk but not being able to make myself look good is really very hard to take. I'd love to be able to run my brush through my hair and put my make-up on instead of having to sit motionless and helpless while others do it for me. I miss nipping into the shower and washing my hair before bedtime. I'm sure that any female reading this will understand exactly what I mean. It was all taken away from my control in the middle of my teenage years and for a teenage girl making herself look good is a pretty high priority!

Mention of the lovely Mo reminds me about all those who have given me brilliant support over the years. It's not just the fact that she's done my hair but that she has made sacrifices and taken time out to make a regular commitment. Others have done their bit and taken time to keep in touch. It's not something that I have assumed or demanded from people but I do appreciate every person who has made an effort. For others, however, my illness has proved more difficult to handle and they have found it awkward to visit me and my family. I understand that.

CHAPTER SIX

An Unforgiving Place

'Five months was a long time to be in that environment.'

As the months passed I became stronger, and eventually Dr Selby decided that it was time to see if I could speak with the tracheotomy. Mum and Dad came up to my room in intensive care with my consultant. He attached a speaking valve to my tracheotomy which would enable me to talk when the air passed through the ventilator. I hadn't heard my voice for five months and I was really apprehensive. The consultant put the valve in and I managed to squeak out a little 'Hi', to the surprise of everyone in the room. It made me jump out of my skin as I had forgotten what my voice had sounded like! Mum and Dad were so happy to hear me again. I can imagine many a time as a child when they did not want to hear another word of my prattling. Now they couldn't be more delighted to hear a simple, two-letter greeting. Spurred on, I practised with the speaking and managed to get back to talking again. It made everything so much easier. Among other things, I could have a proper conversation with my grandparents who were no doubt confused about all that had happened to me. That was great.

Fran: Once Hannah had the speaking valve she could communicate and that was a rarity in intensive care. Most are unconscious and in for a short time. Because Hannah could now talk again she was someone who the staff could identify with and communicate with. Even the chef! She was more like a hospital pet than a patient!

My eating habits were steadily improving. I know people complain about hospital food, but as I got used to eating again, I can honestly say that the food made for me at Alder Hey was delicious! There was a chef who would always think about the patients who were there long term and would let you put in requests for whatever you fancied. I remember some evenings he made me lovely meals like chicken chasseur and duck à l'orange. He was so lovely and would often come and see me and check on how I was.

As the improvements took place I started to take in more of what was around me. There was no getting away from the fact that I was surrounded by very poorly people and five months was a long time to be in that environment. My parents were a constant presence and, inevitably, they made friendships with other families who were suffering their own personal anguish. It is particularly hard to cope when there are children involved.

Some children were just too poorly to survive. Mum, being Mum, supported other grieving families through their heartache. She got to know some of the parents really well and often left my bedside to visit them in another part of intensive care. She was to share in grief on all too many occasions.

Fran: *Supporting so many others was really hard. One mother asked me to hold her baby after she had died. I had talked a lot with the family in Ronald McDonald House. The baby had experienced huge problems.*

Jessica: *We shouldn't have been there. The ward was full of genuinely ill children, some of whom were dying. It wasn't fair on us to be there and for them to see us there. In one sense Hannah wasn't ill and we were there to keep her occupied and entertained. I'm sure that if I was in a situation where my child was dying I wouldn't want us to be around. Mum naturally gravitated towards the families and them to her. That is the kind of the person she is. It's lovely to see. That's her make-up but it put an increasing strain on her shoulders.*

Some time later, a friend of mine applied for a job. It turned out that the woman who interviewed him had a son, Thomas, who had been in Alder Hey at the same time as Hannah. Thomas became the next long-stay ventilation patient after Hannah. We did meet them, but sadly their little boy died. The woman explained to my friend that she still sends Christmas cards to Mum because she was so helpful and kind to her in Alder Hey.

There was a girl next to me who had fallen through a window. Sadly, she did not recover. Then there was the young boy in the room opposite me who had been very poorly. He had been there a while and I remember one afternoon somebody coming and closing my curtain very quickly. I could hear a commotion outside. Later that day I found out that the little boy had suddenly died. It was so strange for me to be in an environment where there were children passing away around me. The gloom that was often felt simply added to the strain of looking after me and I don't know how Mum and Dad coped with it, to be honest. Despite the magnificent support of its staff, the intensive care unit could be such a difficult place to live in. You forget over time how bad it was. I visit the hospital from time to time and although the long corridors and the wards are familiar, as are many of the faces in the staff, it is still hard to recall those dark days.

Fran: *Looking back through rose-tinted spectacles, intensive care seems better than it was. In truth it was horrible.*

You were perpetually in a bubble and had no comprehension of the world outside. You lost all track of time. The television continued to regurgitate hour after hour of light entertainment but the kind of stuff I watched was telling me little about everyday life in the real world. Occasionally, outside events would invade our space. Debbie, Howie's cousin, got married again in the summer of 1999 and we never made the wedding. We were aware of Manchester United playing Bayern Munich in the Champions League final on May 26 1999. A television was brought in so that Dad could watch the match, despite it being the wrong Manchester team involved! Everyone was getting excited. Bayern took an early lead but United came back sensationally with two injury-time goals, from Sheringham and Solskjaer. It was a comeback to match City's own against QPR in the last league game 13 years later, to secure the Premier League.

It was essential that every effort was made to enliven the atmosphere and, believe it or not, I can look back and smile now about many of the things that went on there. It was not all doom and gloom and I cannot believe some of the things that happened. For one thing, I had my belly button pierced! How crazy is that? With the fun provided by some fantastic staff and regular visits from my friends it was possible to produce a party atmosphere on many an occasion.

As I was clearly in for the long haul, I had made myself at home by decorating the hospital room with posters of Robbie Williams and characters from *Friends* and favourite items from home, like soft toys and lava lamps. Our good friend Maurice even brought me a fish tank with two fish in, which really cheered my room up.

After a couple of months I really started to miss my sausage dog, Eric. The nurses had an idea of letting him come in for a visit and I couldn't believe it when the hospital agreed! Before I could see Eric, he had to have swabs taken for infection. The doctors provided my dad with the swabs, but Eric needed a rectal swab and Dad didn't want to do it so, embarrassingly, he asked Martine, our next-door neighbour! Thankfully she agreed. I still can't believe that Dad had the front to ask her! The swabs came back clear and Eric duly came in for a visit. He wasn't allowed up the main staircase so he climbed up the steps of the fire exit and straight into my room which was nearby. It was lovely to see him, but I don't think he enjoyed the experience as I think he thought he was at the vet's!

After what seemed like an age, I was into a recovery process and getting stronger. I was by no means out of the woods and there had been no change on my long-term prognosis, but positive things did begin to happen with more regularity and that gave me hope to cling on to.

CHAPTER SEVEN

Extending My Horizons

'It was really strange seeing everything on the shelves behind my bed.'

I decided that I wanted to carry on with some of the studies that had been disrupted by my falling ill. Just to remind you, I was in Year 10 at school and had already taken my GCSE options. However, some of these subjects were practically based and now beyond my capability, so I just chose three GCSEs that I knew would be possible to complete. Mathematics was an important one to have, as was English, while German was a subject that I particularly enjoyed. There was a Maths teacher already working at the hospital who was able to tutor me and did some English with me as well. However, we didn't know any German teachers so school located a retired German teacher, Jane Copeman, who worked locally.

I clearly remember when Jane first came to meet me. She had grey hair in a bun on the top of her head and the largest green glasses I have ever seen. She seemed so eccentric! When I got to know her I found I was definitely right about the eccentric part, but she is one of the loveliest women I have ever met and we are still friends to this day.

Now aged around 70, Jane still looks and acts exactly the same. She's still as jovial as ever. Mum and I went to see her quite recently. She told Mum that she had got a ramp to help get me into the house, but it turned out to be an ordinary bit of wood which wouldn't have taken the weight of me and my wheelchair, so we stayed in the garden and chatted. I wouldn't have met and kept Jane as a friend had it not been for the illness.

One of the benefits of my studying was that it relieved the monotony of hospital life. Despite the crazy and fun-filled interludes that I have referred to, most of the time it was very uneventful and it was good to get my teeth into something more purposeful. I got regular visits from my tutors and started to enjoy learning again.

One of the nurses suggested that it was time that I stopped wearing pyjamas all the time and that I wore everyday clothes. My first reaction was that I didn't want to start getting dressed. I cannot explain why and I can't really remember my reasoning for wanting to stay in PJs permanently. I do know that I had built up quite a nice collection of attractive pyjamas by this point, though, so that may have had a part to play! I relented and agreed to the nurse's suggestion. I still had some pain in my shoulder so getting dressed was difficult. To make things easier, Mum bought me some cheap clothes and cut them up the back so that I could just put my arms through and then tape them at the back. The nurses would help dress me. I could not get fully dressed. With no control over my bladder and bowels, I had to wear adult nappies all the time. The feed that the nurses were giving me meant that I had an upset stomach constantly and had to get changed often, which wasn't very pleasant.

The steady stream of visitors continued to come to my room, including a number of teachers from St Nicholas. Because of my condition, I don't think that I was able to fully show my gratitude at the time but now, looking back, I cannot thank everyone enough. Every visit showed me that I had not been forgotten about. Mum and Dad's friends were constantly amazing. They helped to make their ordeal that little bit easier and some of Mum's friends would just come and sit with her for hours.

A further sign of progress was when the physiotherapists decided that it was time for me to try and get out of bed, which meant that I needed to get used to sitting up so that my blood pressure would not drop too quickly. We raised the back of the bed gradually over the next few weeks and eventually I was hoisted into an armchair to one side. It was really strange seeing everything on the shelves behind my bed. There were cuddly toys aplenty and dozens of cards with their get-well messages. It was unbelievable. Sitting up was just the strangest feeling and it took me some time to get used to it.

Again at the suggestion of the physiotherapists, I was introduced to a tilt table. This was a type of plinth which had a motor at the back and Velcro straps to secure a person into it. It would then gradually rise to a 90-degree angle to enable a disabled person to stand. The very thought of this made me feel very nervous. I was hoisted on, fastened into place and then the physiotherapists started to gradually increase the angle. The movement had a big effect on me. It made me lose my sight temporarily and my blood pressure again had to be carefully monitored. I used to hate the tilting and could only manage a few minutes at a time. The nurses were always there to calm me down when I started to panic. Following the initial shock, they started to give me medication to control my blood pressure and I soon began to enjoy standing and gradually built up my time on the machine.

It took a number of months to train my inert body to adjust to getting out of bed. It had become so used to lying down and it was strange when I started to get up again. I gradually began having more physiotherapy, which involved daily trips to see the lovely Andrea and Jo. It was really hard work but I enjoyed having a laugh with them as they were great company.

My muscles were still very weak and I was having difficulty holding my head up but it was great to get out of bed. It was one of those landmark moments that appear throughout this book, marking the end of one stage of recovery and the start of the next.

One day the weather was particularly nice and my consultant suggested that it would be a good idea to spend some time outside the confines of the hospital. I was really apprehensive at this prospect but it would be lovely to feel the fresh air and sun on my face again. It had been a long time since I had experienced those simple pleasures. The nurses pushed me through the corridors into parts of Alder Hey that I didn't even know existed. It was a very strange experience to see faces staring at me along the journey. It made me feel really self-conscious and this was the first time that I noticed people looking at me differently. Today this would not bother me at all, but back then I hated it! We got to the front door and, finally, I was outside in the sunshine. It was an amazing moment and seemed like a huge achievement. Above all, it felt unreal.

The next step was to see if I was able to breathe independently of the ventilator. They attached me to an ambulatory bag and watched to see if there was any movement in the bag as I tried to take breaths. The Ambu bag, as it is also known, is a flexible reservoir bag connected by tubing to a face mask and used for artificial ventilation. Nobody really knew what to expect but there was great excitement when I managed without the ventilator for one minute. We practised more and more each day and I think that within a week I was managing about four minutes at a time. From needing a ventilator constantly I have come to no longer rely on one to that extent. That's made a big difference. I can stay off it for quite a long time now, up to 12 hours in fact, and that helps enormously because it means that, for one thing, I don't need to have extra trained people around me at places like work. I'll still go on the ventilator when it suits me because it makes me cope better when I next come off. As a general rule, though, I won't take it with me if I'm going out and that is a big help when planning trips. If it's a particularly long journey then maybe I will include it, but it's unlikely, which is a big improvement on the situation that prevailed back in 1999.

Karen: When Hannah left hospital I recorded in my diary the hours per day that she had achieved off the ventilator.

Day by day I was becoming stronger and healthier and soon it was time for me to be considered for a move away from intensive care.

CHAPTER EIGHT
Heading to High Dependency

'I must have been one of the only patients to have two rooms, one for my clothes!'

The High Dependency Unit (HDU) is a stage between intensive care and the general ward with a staffing ratio to match. Not all hospitals have them; patients would be transferred straight back to the general ward in these cases.

The decision to move me was a good sign but, not for the first time in my story, a positive step in the right direction was about to be knocked sideways. I had come through a really difficult phase in intensive care and had every right to feel happier about finally leaving. However, I started to feel strange.

I began to feel nauseous, in fact, and was convinced that I was hearing noises in my head. I explained what was going on to one of the doctors but nobody understood what might be causing it. Dad picked up from my blood gases that the calcium in my blood had started to rise. However, my usual consultant was on holiday and the consultant who had taken over would not listen to what Dad said. Over the next few weeks the situation worsened. I was hallucinating regularly and feeling very, very sick.

One night this all came to a head. It was the night after two of my friends, Fiona and Rachel, had visited me. Despite my not feeling well, it had been lovely to see them.

I could hear banging noises constantly and they were driving me mad. I explained the noises to the nurses and they thought that it might be the sound of the staff room door as people left the room. They put a note on the door to ask nurses to shut the door quietly. However, the noises were actually in my head and wouldn't go away.

Rosanne visited me at this time and apparently I confided in her that I wanted to be in heaven. It was as if someone else was talking on my behalf. In the evening I had started to get visions that were scaring me. They were very strange and attempting an explanation now is difficult without making it sound like some mad dream. Mum had gone back home to pick up Jessica and Naomi from school. I had Dad staying with me at Ronald McDonald House, as he still did practically every night. He reacted quickly and made an urgent call to Mum at about two in the morning telling her to get to the hospital as fast as she could, as things had turned very serious.

Howie: *I was sitting nearby when Hannah suddenly asked, 'Why have you got goldfish coming out of your hair?' As well as that, she could see a friend's head on the shelf! As if that wasn't enough, Hannah had been watching* Brookside *and while I was sitting with her she recited the whole episode word for word!*

We discovered that my calcium levels, as Dad had suspected, were dramatically high. I know you always think you're right, Dad, but I'll give you credit for this one! I was experiencing an episode of something called hypercalcaemia. This is apparently a condition which can befall people who are immobile as the calcium from their bones is not being used up and is secreted into the bloodstream. All this explained what I had said to Rosanne as well as the hallucinations and noises.

I just remember waking up the next morning and feeling totally wiped out. With what little energy I had left I looked down and saw that all my groin area was completely filled with lines and drips. Dad told me what had happened and I realised what had been building up during the previous weeks.

Thankfully, I recovered from the episode and continued along an upward path. After five months in intensive care it was finally decided that I would be ready to move to the High Dependency Unit. This was great news, obviously, but to counter that feeling I was also very apprehensive as I had become comfortable with all the staff in the intensive care ward and used to my room. Once again, the worrier in Hannah Rose came to the surface!

Moving day arrived and I was to be transferred to Ward 2. It was newly built and I was given a double room to myself to accommodate all of my belongings. I must have been one of the only patients to have two rooms, one for my clothes! More or less everybody on the HDU had their own individual room. It was really strange to be away from the intensive care ward that I had got to know so well. I wasn't completely out of the woods yet and there were still very sick children on this ward with me.

The day was really quite stressful for me. Whilst I was being wheeled in my wheelchair from intensive care to the HDU, my catheter came out, so when I arrived in my new 'home' the first thing that had to happen was to have it re-inserted. This wasn't the best of starts and I remember feeling distraught as my first meeting with my new nurses was when they were inserting the catheter. I used to hate that process so much as it felt degrading. Even though I had no feeling in that area the thought of what was going on made me shudder and having a new set of nurses sorting it out was something that I just did not need.

The new surroundings took a bit of getting used to but I started to get to know the nurses quickly. The medical staff in Alder Hey were consistently brilliant. I became really close to a lot of them and we could always have a good giggle about things. I loved being with some of the younger nurses and we would gossip about shared interests. They became firm friends.

I was still dependent on a vanload of machinery and there was plenty of pain yet to be suffered along the way. A battery of tests and checks remained a regular part of everyday life. A tube was regularly put down my throat into my lungs to clear the mucus as I got really bad chests.

After a few weeks on the new ward it was decided that I would be able to have some hydrotherapy, which involved the use of water for pain relief and treating illness. I was really excited about this and couldn't wait to get into the pool. I was slightly apprehensive, though, as I knew that I would have to put my trust in people to take me into the water. It sounds silly now but one of the biggest concerns I had was having a bowel accident in the water! I also remember feeling really embarrassed in my swimming costume. By the time I got down to the pool I was really nervous but once I got in it felt amazing. The physiotherapist would move my arms in the water to try and strengthen my muscles. It felt as though my arms could move slightly as I experienced weightlessness in the water. I really enjoyed the sensation and continued to look forward to the weekly sessions.

Gradually I began to realise how much I needed help with dressing and with my personal care. I suppose it was another sign of my progress as I was taking in more of what was happening around me. I was beginning to feel really self-conscious about my body and, in particular, the fact that I could not go the toilet. I started to find these things very difficult to cope with and always made it clear that I wanted my body to be covered with a towel and not exposed whilst I was having a wash. This is still the same today. It was also decided that I would have my catheter removed in favour of a more permanent solution. I had a procedure done to insert a suprapubic catheter. This is a hollow, flexible tube that is used to drain urine from the bladder. It is inserted through a cut in the tummy, a few inches below the navel, and has a number of advantages. It is more comfortable and less likely to give you an infection than other catheters. It is also less invasive and gave me more dignity.

My friends continued to be fantastic and visits increased after I left intensive care. Either teachers or mums would bring them to see me on Friday evenings. How good is that?

Lizzy: *Our mums would take us in rotation and either go and see Fran or drop us off and go to do some shopping. We would often arrive laden with goodies, usually chocolate brownies!*

Anna: *Oh, the highlight of the week, without a doubt. It was either fish and chips or a McDonald's and the room would always smell of one or the other.*

Kate: *We nattered away and listened to Robbie Williams.*

Karen: *Definitely the Friday night weekly routine in Year 11. After getting the food from over the road we would argue around*

Hannah's bed about whether we would watch TFI Friday *or* The Simpsons. *I think* The Simpsons *usually won!*

Anna: *After the telly programmes we would watch the film* Dirty Dancing *and keep rewinding to the scene where you can see an inch of Patrick Swayze's bum!*

Susan: *As well as doing things together, we also had private chats with Hannah one-to-one. She liked that.*

Rosanne: *We saw Hannah more often on the High Dependency Unit. She had stabilised and was more able to have regular visitors. She used to enjoy the one-to-one sessions and often used them to express her deepest sorrows.*

Celia: *I remember going to Alder Hey and pulling up outside the hospital to drop Susan off. About ten minutes later Howie came down and started talking to my dad. I remember thinking what a scary place the hospital must be. I was always outside, either dropping off or picking up with my parents. I never went in because Hannah was Susan's friend at that time. Ironically, I would be there myself in 2001.*

Celia had a brain tumour and her family have had to go through their own agony. They have been brilliant supporters for me. Despite a difference of about eight years in age a close friendship has grown between Celia and me over recent years.

Celia: *I wasn't in for anything like as long as Hannah. I had a lot of treatment done at the Walton Centre, a specialist unit for neurosciences, but a lot of my chemotherapy was done at Alder Hey. Our friendship grew after Hannah came home. I did some fund-raising at school and one of the tutors brought me round to drop the money off at Hannah's. I started to get to know her better from then onwards. We have both been through so much at a young age and it brought us closer.*

Before the school year finished, my friends put together tapes of jokes to cheer me up. They made cakes and I also got a video sent to me. Each person in my class took turns to send me crazy messages from a chair in the middle of the classroom. The boys who I said I'd fancied would go bright red! The messages would feature school events like sports day and they would tell me that they would try particularly hard for me. It's really, really funny in places but also very emotional. Many said that they would come and visit me but of course they didn't – that's just human nature. It's not their fault. A number commented, 'See you in September.' Unfortunately, that was never to happen. I used to get really excited about what was going on and wanted to know about everything but still felt sad that I was missing out.

I think back to school days a lot and when I look at home videos I see my hands, arms and legs moving freely and it's so strange. Also the home videos that we made show me moving around doing normal things. It's like stepping back through a mirror and is the closest I can get to seeing what I used to be like without actually re-creating it. It's like looking at a stranger and as time goes on it makes me worry that I might forget what I was like. I don't want to forget and this book will help me avoid that. Videos can be so sad to watch, though. Apart from me being able to see myself as I was, my grandparents are filmed looking younger and more agile and it's sad to think that they are not like that anymore. These are images of a family blissfully unaware of what was to hit them. Reminiscing about home and school has always been important to me. It's all part of my ability to cope with what life has thrown at me.

One of the more bizarre visits to Alder Hey was from comedian Syd Little, the more serious half of the comedy double act 'Little and Large' who were very popular in the late 1970s and 1980s. Sue and Dave knew Syd and happened to mention to him that I was in hospital. I didn't know about this and a few days later Syd arrived at Alder Hey with a bunch of flowers in hand after travelling by bus to get there! He was appearing in pantomime in Liverpool at the time. I was a little embarrassed as I didn't really know of him that well, but it was a lovely surprise. It certainly caused quite a stir amongst the nurses, most of whom were old enough to remember him. Before long I had a signed photograph of Little and Large on my wall!

Months later, after I had returned home, the house phone rang. My mum answered and brought it to me. 'It's Syd for you,' she said. I was racking my brains trying to think of a Syd that I knew but couldn't. I was really surprised when I heard his enthusiastic voice say, 'Hi Hannah, it's Syd Little here'. Syd had rung to ask me if he could include me in his autobiography. I didn't mind at all and was actually really excited about being in a book. Now I am featuring in one as the leading role and he is in mine!

Karen: *Hannah, as we all know, is obsessed with celebrities and used to get to meet those who visited Alder Hey. It seemed to me like there was a footballer or a celebrity in there every other week!*

There was a little armchair in my room and the nurses began sitting me in it for longer periods of the day, which was good as it made a change from the bed. I was fitted for my own wheelchair. I can't really recall much about this other than that it felt very uncomfortable when it arrived.

As I had now sampled the fresh air outside Alder Hey, the next step was to go for a trip out of the hospital grounds. We kept our ambitions limited and the nurses and Mum thought it would be good to have a trip to Sainsbury's round the corner. I was so worried about it when I got into a black cab in my wheelchair with Mum and a nurse. It was really strange being in a car after five months in hospital. We soon arrived at the supermarket and all I could think about was how I didn't want to get out of the car. The thought of seeing and meeting members of the public was making me panic. I waited in the car for about ten minutes whilst the nurse popped in to the shop to get some things. We then drove back to the hospital. Recalling these activities makes me realise where I am now. I am out and about every single day and have been abroad a number of times. It is important to keep this perspective clear in my mind because it shows how far I have come on my journey.

Just before Christmas 1999, a nurse came to speak to me and asked whether I was a fan of Liverpool Football Club. I think I said 'Yes' but, in truth, wasn't really a huge football fan at that time. She said that there was a chance to meet the Liverpool players and asked whether I would like to go for a trip out. This was going to be my first major excursion away from the hospital. Two of the nurses and Mum came with me. Dad, despite being a Manchester City fan, was secretly disappointed that he had to work. Mum bought me a coat and turned up with this horrible bomber jacket which I complained about big style at first. I was wondering what the players would think of it but then eventually conceded that it would indeed keep me warm!

The following day we went to the Liverpool training ground at Melwood in the West Derby area of the city. I honestly didn't recognise any of the players except for Michael Owen who I was so excited to meet! Everyone was lovely and spent a lot of time talking to us. We got pictures with all the players and they signed a football for me. I took a Michael Owen calendar and, unashamedly, asked if he could sign every page of it so that I could give them out to friends! I also felt quite embarrassed as Mum went on and on about being an avid fan of Manchester City! It was a lovely day and, even though I was exhausted by the end of it, I felt good about having some time out of the hospital.

With all this happening, Mum and Dad started to look for a wheelchair-accessible vehicle. They particularly wanted to get me home for a few hours on Christmas Day. This was to be the first time that I had returned home since leaving the house to go to the doctor's back in May.

CHAPTER NINE

Preparing to Come Home

'... a complex and detailed process.'

We all knew that it was going to be a difficult day, but Mum and Dad felt that it was important that we kept some semblance of normality on Christmas Day, even if it was just being at home together for a few hours to celebrate the festive season. We had to take one of the nurses from the ward with us as I needed some antibiotics and she was the only one who could give them to me. We did not get a vehicle sorted out in time so I returned to Chester Road in a black cab and had to travel in it sideways as there was no room for me to sit frontwards, the 'right way round'! It was so strange being in a car for that length of time and arriving at my house was really surreal. I cast my mind back to that day so long ago when I had walked out and into the car for the appointment with the doctor. Seven months had passed since then. I don't remember the Christmas 'celebrations' all that well but I can picture dinner with a complete stranger sitting at the table with us in the shape of the nurse! Definitely the worst bit of the day was leaving home again and going back to hospital.

That New Year's Eve marked the millennium and I remember being on my bed in the High Dependency Unit with all my family around and drinking champagne out of plastic cups! We watched all the celebrations on television. Plans were in motion to get me back home again. Mum and Dad finally purchased a van which was a bit shabby, but we knew it would be useful to make the journey to and from hospital. I started to come back on a Sunday afternoon and would have my evening meal at home before returning to Alder Hey later. I absolutely hated returning to hospital but after a few weeks we got into a routine. It was then decided that it might be good to broaden my outlook and have a trip out to do some shopping. Mum, one of the nurses and I went to my 'favourite place in the whole world', the Trafford Centre. I just remember buying some new trainers and some tops and it was great being able to choose my own after such a long period.

My 16th birthday came and it felt strange that I was going to be marking the event in hospital. What a day it was, though, as all my best friends turned up to see me as a surprise. It was such a nice thing to do and it would not have felt right celebrating my birthday without them.

Karen: *When Hannah became ill we had just started to gain more independence and had begun to go out. Hitting 16 is a big time in your life and, suddenly, Hannah wasn't there to share it with us after being through the teenage years together. I think we all found that hard.*

While I was getting the chance to catch up with friends, Mum's friends were a great support for her. Here are two of them, Sue Mitchell and Chris Mather:

Sue: *I tried to go down every week, to support Fran as much as anything. I used to have to sit in the waiting room for ages before being allowed into intensive care as things might be happening on the ward. People related to other patients would often come in to the room upset. I would just sit for a couple of hours. One time Hannah was really poorly with green mucus coming out of mouth. It wasn't nice to see her so ill, but she always kept her spirits up even though she would have felt awful. I always tried to make a fuss of Jessica and Naomi as well as it must have been so hard on them. We would go to Ronald McDonald's to eat or have a cup of tea. We would also come down as a family to get a pizza takeaway to eat with the Roses.*

Chris: *I usually went on a Friday afternoon to give Fran a break. She would go for a coffee in the café or to ring family and friends* *while I kept Hannah company. Like Sue, I would often have to wait if Hannah was toileting. There would be curtains round her bed and it could take up to an hour so I just sat and read the paper until Fran came out. She has been so supportive of me at difficult times so I know how it really can cheer you up when a friendly face walks in.*

I also enjoyed seeing Sarah and Stuart Dornford-May. Stuart would always make me laugh with his infectious cackle, whilst the Hynes and Hendry families would regularly pitch up with picnics and set their stall out across the room! The Storeys were another supportive family.

Every visit provided welcome relief and support for Mum and Dad. It was a physically demanding schedule as they tried to balance my needs with those of my sisters. Dad, of course, was still at work. It must have been so strange and difficult for my family to come to terms with my illness. There would be many days when Mum would be with me until about half two in the afternoon before driving the 26 miles to pick the girls up from school in Hartford and then driving back again, a schedule she kept up for 15 gruelling months.

Naomi: *Mum picked us up on Greenbank Road after school and she wasn't always on time. We'd often get lots of verbal abuse from local children and teenagers as we waited. We'd be called 'Bible Bashers' because we went to St Nicholas! Mum sent a friend to pick us up once. There was a dead cat on the road. The friend picked it up in front of everyone and put it at the side of the road shouting dramatically, 'Nobody look!' Jess and I were so embarrassed. Our friend Maurice also acted as chauffeur. To be honest we could have walked home. It wasn't that far and we'd have been quicker doing that. Mum would always make excuses for being late like there were cows crossing the road. She'd take about an hour every day, which was really annoying when we had to stand around waiting.*

Jessica: *Maurice came to pick us up in his Triumph Stag, the kind of sports car that you don't see too often at the school gates! He's a lovely guy who has done a lot for our family but that* *was embarrassing. There was already quite a bit of attention on Naomi and myself anyway, which I wasn't exactly comfortable with. I hated being marked out as different in any way.*

Fran: *I used to leave Hannah at about half two. She never wanted me to go, but as I raced across Runcorn Bridge I also felt guilty about picking Jessica and Naomi up late.*

Chris: *I helped pick the girls up from school. I wanted to take the pressure off Fran so that she wasn't rushing home in the traffic. Many a time she would be waiting for a consultant to come or go and could easily be late so she gave me a ring and I was happy to oblige.*

Fran: *I'm ashamed to admit that I don't remember much about Naomi's first year in high school.*

Jessica: *It was really difficult for Naomi when she started at St Nicholas. I'd been there a couple of years and already got my own friends. I had gone with another pupil from primary school so there was always that familiar face around as I settled in. Naomi went alone. It was the worst timing ever, to be honest. School wanted to make a fuss and talk about it whereas she and I just wanted to talk about anything but.*

Jess was very protective of Naomi. Mum and Dad weren't there, neither was I. During her first year at St Nicholas, people kept coming up to Naomi and asking about me. One person had a charity box and asked her to give some money for a girl called Hannah! She didn't know that Naomi was my sister. They were saying prayers for me in chapel services at school.

Jessica: *Mum and Dad just couldn't be everywhere at once, but they still kept our lives as normal as possible with birthday parties and such. I just don't know how they've come through it. Unbelievable. They're just brilliant, aren't they?*

There are many occasions when I have thought about how strong my mum and dad's relationship must be. Many would simply not have coped with all this upheaval to their lives. I saw one of the other Alder Hey patients quite recently and she told me that her parents had split up, as had others. It is all so sad, but it is inevitably going to happen when partnerships are placed under so much stress. Thankfully, it did not happen to my mum and dad.

Fran: Howie is incredibly tolerant. A lot of men in his position simply would not hack it. We met one family in hospital where the husband just couldn't cope anymore and left. We have always taken the view that as parents you just get on with it and support the best you can. Maybe we've been too supportive at times. Over the years I'd say that I've taken more chances than Howie. He's more the worrying kind whereas I would say, 'Go for it!'

I was still having physiotherapy and hydrotherapy and managing a few hours off the ventilator as I became stronger each day. We were looking forward and reaching the point at which we started to consider me leaving hospital and returning home permanently.

'Straightforward' is not a word that I can easily apply to my life and getting me home was far from straightforward. If only I could have packed a bag and headed down the open road back into Cheshire. In fact, it was to prove a complex and detailed process that had to be planned in minute detail both in Liverpool and at home in Hartford.

Mum and Dad had already contacted Maurice, who was a builder by trade, to physically adapt our house. What used to be the garage was to be converted into my bedroom, totally accessible with a bathroom and a ceiling track hoist. Ironically, despite the massive amount of money which would be pledged to my future care, no assistance was given to modify the house for me so Mum and Dad had to pay.

Caring for me at home was to be a new experience for everybody involved because there had not been any cases in my local area of paediatric patients coming home on long-term ventilation and needing a care package. A nurse coordinator came out to visit me in Alder Hey. She would oversee and manage the care team that would look after me at home.

I remember the first day I met her as clear as anything. I was sitting on my bed eating a chicken salad lunch. Dad was with me. There was a knock on the door. The coordinator came over to me and spoke in a very slow, deliberate voice as if I would not be able to understand her: 'Hello, Hannah, how are you?' It wasn't the best of starts. She went on to explain that the Primary Care Trust had begun advertising for a team that would support my every need back at home. Trusts manage the provision of primary care services in a specific area. These include services provided by doctors' surgeries, opticians and dental practices. There are over 150 of them across England.

As I didn't know anything about this process I was just happy to sit back and let others organise it on my behalf. I don't think I had any notion of what was going on or that I would need 24-hour care. Yet again, it all seemed unreal and it was as if I was locked inside a bubble while all these plans were being made. I can remember looking forward to going home, but I can't really remember being overly excited about it. In my head I just thought that I would go back, things would return to normal and I would be back with my friends in school. Wrong! Reality had still not yet hit me but when it did it was with the force of a knockout punch!

We did a trial night at home and the ward sister came with me. It was so weird. Here I was in the garage! Admittedly, it had been painted and Maurice had done a great job but it felt so cold, probably because in my mind I was still thinking of it as the garage and the conversion into my cosy room had not been fully completed.

Howie: Just before Hannah became ill we had an extension made to the kitchen, to make a dining area. We'd decorated the area and bought a new table and chairs. We now needed an entrance into the former garage, Hannah's new bedroom, and the recently completed work had to be dismantled to make access to the new room. I remember thinking what a great job Maurice had done creating a beautifully decorated bedroom out of the garage. Then the ceiling tracking and the hoist were put in and I became all too aware that it wasn't just an attractive extension that Maurice had created but a home for my disabled daughter.

As night came, everyone else went upstairs to bed, leaving me alone with my carer. I hated the thought of being downstairs although I know a lot of people do sleep on the ground floor. I didn't get much sleep that night!

A month or two later I was shown a pile of application forms from people who had applied to be my carers. I had a look through them but, in all honesty, I didn't really have any concept of the importance of who I would end up choosing to care for me. I remember looking for common interests with me that they might have indicated in the forms. I saw that one of the ladies was a big Robbie Williams fan so that was enough to get her an interview! I was only 16 at the time and I had absolutely no experience of looking through application forms, interviewing or employing people. It was way out of my comfort zone.

A multi-disciplinary team was formed. The NHS drove the process and organised a series of meetings, normally involving up to 16 people at a time but I think that the record round the table was 23! It was becoming a lengthy and tedious process. My heart wasn't really in it and, to be honest, I didn't understand a lot of what was happening around me. I just went with the flow from inside my large bubble. Naomi clearly did not appreciate the seriousness of the meetings:

Naomi: *Thanks for bringing that up, Hannah! One day I thought I would surprise Mum and Dad and hide under Hannah's bed. I didn't realise that they were going to have a meeting with the coordinator and all the carers. I stuck it out for about half an hour then had to crawl out! On another occasion I hid behind a chair in the corner before jumping out. Crazy!*

A huge budget was allocated to recruit staff and provide the necessary equipment. A short list was drawn up and a visit was arranged for all the carers to come and meet me in hospital. I can picture myself sitting in my room on the ward with a circle of prospective carers around me. Some were young, others middle-aged and I felt quite overwhelmed and awkward. I didn't really know what to talk about! They were all very nice and chatty, but I still didn't grasp what was going on at the time. Some of the applicants dropped out as maybe it wasn't what they had expected. However, others stayed and ended up getting a job. A team of eight plus a team leader were recruited to look after me at home.

Around June 2000 it was decided that I should visit school. Mum and Dad went with me from Alder Hey and we spent half a day at St Nicholas. Nobody really knew what to say. I sat in a lesson, English I think.

Karen: When there was the possibility of Hannah visiting St Nicholas we had to keep it a secret in case it didn't happen as she was nervous about going back, even for a short visit.

I was positioned next to another pupil's desk and it felt really strange. I felt moments of sheer panic, something that was to return to haunt me from time to time in different places. In these situations I cannot move or breathe properly but I have to deal with it and then move on. As Mum said, 'You have to sink or swim, Hannah.' I think that a lot of the problem stems from not wanting to draw attention to myself. If I know that I cannot get out of a situation quickly and that the only way out is for everyone to look at me, being in that sort of position definitely increases my anxiety. I have to be careful when I am in large groups like at a wedding and make sure that I am comfortable with where I am in the crowd.

I remember getting a panic attack when I first went to the cinema after leaving hospital. It was at Cheshire Oaks and we went to see *About a Boy*, the comedy film with Hugh Grant.. I had only watched the first ten minutes and couldn't go on any further. I felt scared in the dark and got worried that I couldn't shout out if I needed help. Another occasion was when we were visited by family friends who we had met in Minorca years ago when I was 13. They came round to the house to see how I was and I had a massive panic attack and had to leave the living room.

It also happened when I went back to Grandma and Grandpa's house for the first time – in fact I still find that hard. It's difficult when I think of the good times I spent there and now I can't run up and down the stairs like I used to. There are rooms upstairs that I'll never go back into. It's hard to go back to houses that I've visited as an able-bodied person.

When we got back to Alder Hey after visiting school, Mum found a note from the coordinator: 'Hannah, I've been tidying up your room and I would like you to sort the following things ...' I still had Christmas presents around ready to give to people who I had not seen for a while and also all my belongings. The note had been written to me as if I could physically do the tidying up! What had already proved to be a difficult day had become worse because we had returned to that. Mum was really angry. The coordinator had gone through all my stuff and asked things like, 'Why have you got so many pairs of jeans?' What business is it of hers how many pairs of jeans I have? It was really bizarre. If that had happened now I would have reacted differently and made my feelings a lot clearer. Back then, I was just young and naive and let it be.

Fran: The lady, who was not tracheotomy-trained, stayed behind on the ward when Hannah visited school. She had no understanding when she wrote the letter that the room had been Hannah's home for months. Did it really matter whether Hannah had ten pairs of jeans?

Over the next few weeks there was a more concerted push to get me home. I started to come back and stay overnight. Those initial visits are fairly clear in my mind, but strangely, I don't actually remember much about the day when I finally severed my link with Alder Hey and moved back into Hartford. I remember the packing up part, though, and we went to Costco for a massive cake for the nurses. We also thanked all the brilliant physiotherapists by taking them out to the Chinese restaurant across the road. We felt they had been exceptionally kind. One of them, Andrea, got married in Manchester and we were all invited.

And so, finally, we drove away from Alder Hey after 481 long days.

CHAPTER TEN

Returning with the Back-up Team

'Family life could never be normal again.'

I came back home on 23 August 2000 having gone into hospital on 20 May 1999. Five of those 15 months had been spent in intensive care. The May date is the birthday of my friend Helen so I always remember the day it all began every time she has her birthday. As each year passes by I find that I am not making a big deal of the anniversaries, particularly if they coincide with a period when I'm busy and doing purposeful things. I focus on what I'm doing rather than dwell on what has happened.

The 12th anniversary, in May 2011, proved to be a very difficult milestone because it found me on my bed and not in a good place. I got really upset, as did my dad. Anyway, more of the horrible 2011 later... I also know that there will be a particularly stressful anniversary to face in 2014 because, when I reach the age of 30, I will enter a period in my life when I will have been disabled for longer than I've been able-bodied. Naomi and I were talking recently and she said, 'Imagine if you'd never got ill...' and that got us thinking. She brought up the point that in her lifetime I had been disabled longer than I had been able-bodied. She didn't mean anything by it, but nevertheless, what she said was a stark reality check. My situation was permanent.

Coping with a team of helpers constantly for 13 years has been an incredibly major issue and it's difficult to believe that there was a time when they weren't there. The invasion of our family privacy has had huge implications for all of us and it began from the moment the first carer stepped through the front door. Family life would never be normal again. Others were sharing our space and we couldn't do anything about it.

If we had a family argument, Mum would ask us to stop because the carers could hear us. This annoyed Jess, who would say, quite rightly, 'So what? This is our house.' I began to make it clear to new appointments that it was a family environment and that should be respected. I asked them to knock before coming into a room because there's nothing worse than a carer barging in when you might be having a deep conversation with Mum or Dad. You often want to have a good chat and can't because you are worried the carers can overhear. No privacy. It must be particularly hard for Dad. Not only does he have four women in his family to put up with but also a whole team of female carers!

I had a little bell for my safety which could ring upstairs in Mum and Dad's room in an emergency. Only you didn't want it to ring out loud in the middle of the night. It was scary. Sometimes a carer would have to go upstairs and knock on the bedroom door. That was really hard for Mum and Dad. They would have a stranger knocking on their bedroom door. Who wants that?

What I found really hard to get used to at home was when we said goodnight. I'm a 28-year-old young woman, I know, but I still like a goodnight kiss. Dad in particular found it difficult. If I wanted a hug at bedtime and Dad gave me one, he would jump straight off the bed when a carer walked in. It made him feel really uncomfortable.

Having my personal needs attended to by others was really hard. With two lifeless arms I was no longer able to do the host of everyday tasks that others take for granted. Particularly difficult was toileting. This is the most personal of acts, but when you are helpless to manage it yourself, relying on others can be embarrassing and upsetting. I worried about having wind; I remember at one point in the early days I was really windy in my stomach and it woke me up. Two young nurses were looking after me. They didn't know I was awake so they started giggling when they heard me making the 'wind noises'. I just lay in bed feeling so embarrassed by it and was close to tears. If it happened now I would tell them to shut up but back then it was a very sensitive subject for a teenage girl.

I constantly resisted efforts to brush my teeth or feed me. I used to find it hard to accept that someone else was there and actually paid to do these things. I just couldn't get used to personal care being done by others, which must have been quite hard for the carers as well.

Feeding has always been particularly difficult. I think it's probably just something to do with me because I've not met many people who've shared the same problem. Sometimes I might just want to eat and watch something on the television by myself, but having to be constantly fed by someone else means that I always feel obliged to strike up a conversation when perhaps I don't want to.

I must stress that I was not completely house-bound. Carers were able to go out with me in my adapted van and this allowed me to go to the shops, for instance, and get away from the four walls that surrounded me.

Naomi: I can remember more about Hannah being at home than when she was at hospital, particularly when she first came home. My home life got turned upside down. That's probably why I've got worse memories of it. It went from being used to having me and Jess, Mum and Dad in the house to having Hannah back and carers going backwards and forwards. They were big changes. It was really embarrassing coming down in pyjamas with strange people walking around, but now I am used to it.

Fran: We all worked towards getting Hannah home, but we didn't really appreciate how difficult it was going to be from then on. Coming home and setting up with the carers was a massive issue. The personal intrusion hit us in a big way and I cannot believe how well Jess and Naomi have turned out considering how much their lives have been affected. In the early days with the carers, we didn't know the boundaries and were feeling our way with them. There have been many issues along the way but, to be fair, the trust had not had anyone like Hannah before. If Hannah had died things would never have been the same again and we would have felt an enormous loss. However, because she was still alive, our lives would still be affected forever.

Jessica: I had a couple of years getting used to the new arrangement at home, then I went to university. By then it was a kind of escape for me; I really felt it in those terms. I would come home once a month or so, nothing like as often as I do now.

The day after I got home was the Thursday when the GCSE results came out. You will remember that I had chosen three subjects to follow while at Alder Hey. I had also taken the examinations in hospital. There was a sign on my door with a very clear message: 'SILENCE'. Little children on the ward were wishing me luck. It was obviously far from normal examination conditions. At certain points, the lunch trolley would arrive and we would have to stop. The Maths was particularly difficult because it involved drawing diagrams. Mrs Cowell, who I still see a lot, had a protractor and ruler and sat on my bed as I gave her precise instructions for my answers. Mrs Cooper did English Language with me and that was easier to organise. The German was also more straightforward. I dictated answers on some parts and spoke my oral piece into a microphone just as I would have done at school. In the weeks before the test, the nurses had put the parts of my oral on bits of paper round the room so that I could keep practising and reminding myself of the key words.

We felt that it was important that I should go to school and collect my results so that I could share in the excitement and happiness of my friends. The thought of experiencing this day and being like everybody else was one of the reasons why I had taken the tests in the first place. As we entered St Nicholas, some people saw us and were taken by surprise, not knowing what to say. The headteacher walked up and said congratulations!. He wasn't wearing his shorts this time! It was well-meaning of him, but he didn't know that I hadn't got my results at that stage.

When I did get them I was so thrilled. This was a little bit of normality for me because I was receiving the dreaded envelope just like countless other students across the country on that August morning and experiencing the same nerves and excitement prior to seeing my results. The only difference was that I was unable to rip the envelope open myself. There were no special arrangements or ceremony, which was fine by me.

I just asked to go somewhere quiet to find out my results but cannot remember where. Not to worry. I got an A* for German, a B in Maths and a C in English. I just could not believe the Maths result! I'll swear to this day that if I had not got ill and not been able to work with a tutor I would have failed that exam. Every cloud…! Dad had failed his Maths examination years ago himself, which really amused me. I was so pleased to get some passes 'in the bag' and rang Helen up as she had just got her results as well.

The Northwich Guardian photographer and reporter came to record the event. There I was on the front of the paper! I so hated my hair in that picture. My friends came back to my house afterwards and we celebrated.

> **Kate:** *We certainly did! Celebrating the GCSEs was lovely. We had a party on a really sunny day. We were so proud of Hannah's achievement.*

> **Lizzy:** *I have forgotten about most of the hospital stuff. What I definitely do remember is that when Hannah came home we had a big party. We sat in the back garden with a bottle of cider brought by Karen. Hannah seemed really happy that day.*

I was… but a bit guilty about swigging the cider! I loved the party and also remember as clear as day that the family had a celebration meal. There was a happy mood around the table, interrupted by the sound of the doorbell which signalled the arrival of the next carer to start a night shift. It was something that we would have to get used to.

I began to adjust to a home life quite different from the one that I had left. It was difficult because of the magnitude of the change. I still had many medical issues surrounding me and was reliant on a lot of machinery, regular tests and medication. There was always the fear of an unexpected twist of fortune and a setback was heading my way…

Several weeks after getting home I suddenly started to go bright red and couldn't breathe properly. There was also a distinctive metallic taste in my mouth. My blood pressure was rising and this was a quite different set of symptoms to anything

I had experienced before so we played safe and phoned the doctor. It was a Saturday. We were told to expect a visit within the next two hours. After half an hour things were getting so bad that we decided to ring 999 instead. An ambulance crew arrived and, reluctantly, I prepared for a return to hospital. Breathing had become very difficult so I needed manual assistance with the ambulatory bag. The hospital trip was clearly for the best. The paramedics didn't know how to deal with all my 'bagging' (assisted breathing) so Dad travelled in the back of the ambulance to help out with the ambulatory bag. The ambulance driver wasn't holding back on the accelerator –we were pelting along! I was on the trolley and Dad was standing pumping the air into me while one of the ambulance men held on to him for dear life at such a high speed. If it wasn't such a serious situation, I swear we could so easily have burst out laughing!

Leighton Hospital is in Crewe, a few miles to the south of home. The Lewis Hamilton wannabe behind the wheel sped up to the front entrance, where we were met by something like another scene from *Casualty*! Tipped off about my condition, a medical team was ready to take over and in I went for tests. Between the hospital and the Spinal Injuries Unit at Southport they decided that I had probably got something called autonomic dysreflexia, which can be considered a medical emergency requiring immediate attention. To put it more simply, it is connected with over-activity in the nervous system which causes excessively high blood pressure. It can lead to seizures, stroke and even death. There are a number of symptoms such as sweating and blotchiness and the pain inside your head can be horrendous. Autonomic dysreflexia affects people with spinal cord injuries or dysfunctions. No wonder all the stops were pulled out to get me there!

Southport recommended a drug we'd never had before, but one that we should have had prescribed already! In fact, I carry it all the time now and if the autonomic dysreflexia flares up again, which it has on several occasions, I take the medication and it lowers my blood pressure again. We couldn't get it immediately first time because the pharmacist wasn't there, it being a Saturday. My condition started to improve, but an hour or two later I was admitted to a side room on the ward as there were no beds available in intensive care. Mum and Dad had to set the ventilator up and nurses were coming in saying, 'That's interesting, what does it do?' I thought that things worked the other way round and we were the ones who asked the questions! Anyway, we spent the night in hospital, but I was allowed home the next day.

Howie: *It was a one-off episode with a happy ending, but nevertheless, it showed a worrying lack of knowledge among certain professionals.*

I started back at school on September 4, so there wasn't much of a gap between coming home and resuming my education. I have to say, St Nicholas were brilliant and they had built a ramp especially for me to access the building. I was now going into the Sixth Form, of course. Apart from the half-day visit three months before, this was the first time that I had been back in class for about 16 months. As I took stock of the situation, I thought how the boys had had such massive growth spurts since I had last seen them!

The first day was understandably strange but I managed. However, the second proved much more stressful because I had one of my panic attacks. It was as if I could not recognise the school that had given me so much happiness and I couldn't believe that it was me that all this had happened to. Perhaps I was expecting too much of myself, but it felt like I was in some bizarre dream. Mum came for me and, as she drove me home, we did a detour, ending up in a lay-by in the nearby village of Whitegate. We both sobbed. Our emotions came out in bucketloads. It was all too much for both of us. I have always loved being at school. Prior to my illness I was motivated to work hard for my exams and had a water sports holiday to look forward to with my school friends. Now it had all gone wrong and this really hurt me.

Mum had also started back at her own school after a long period away. She was still at Greenbank Residential School. Her school was about a mile down the road so I felt that she wasn't far away. On many occasions, I needed her at home for one thing or another and she would never let me down. She would rush to my side, sort things out and go back. I had a pang of guilt every time we had to make the call.

As I tried to come to terms with my new life, I took a turn for the worse and went rapidly downhill.

CHAPTER ELEVEN

Confined to My Room

'I would often lie awake crying uncontrollably.'

It happened shortly after the start of the new school year. It is difficult to work out how and why but my spirits fell dramatically. My family and friends had all returned to their own work and studies. I realised that I could no longer do the same. School had planned for me but it had been an inauspicious start. I had perhaps been in denial and expecting my problems to be short-term. Now it was becoming very clear that this was far from the case. I was still in the springtime of my life and there were many years stretching ahead of me but I was no longer able to follow the plan that I had set out countless times in my mind. It seemed that others were moving off down the career path and leaving me behind. This realisation hit me hard.

Beyond that, I cannot remember what caused the dip. I suppose that by trying to block it out of my mind at the time I ended up remembering precious little. It must be a natural bodily reaction. What I can tell you is that shock and depression hit me in a big way and I was confined to my bedroom for the best part of the next two years. It is difficult to describe the physical and mental torture that I felt during that time and I really hit new depths. I was pretty close to reaching rock bottom.

When I get depressed it makes me feel more vulnerable. I felt in a living hell and strapped to the bed. Anxiety and despair overcame me in waves. I needed my mum to be near me all the time and asked her if she really had to go to work. Yet again, it must have been hard for her and Dad because every time I've demanded something, they've always responded as best they can. Even all these years later, I don't think that I've appreciated them as much as I should have.

I locked myself away in my bedroom and my inability to move for a long period led to me experiencing my first pressure sore. Pressure sores develop when compression of the skin in one part of the body cuts off the blood supply and usually occur when someone sits or lies in one position for too long. Starting from a red area of skin, sores can develop rapidly. Sometimes fat and muscle layers under the skin can be destroyed to such an extent that bones are exposed. Sadly, others were to follow, one of which was particularly nasty so it's best that you are not eating your tea when I describe that one later in the book!

I lay on my bed in a sorry state. I wasn't eating or drinking properly for long periods of time. Anti-depressants were prescribed. I would often lie awake until three o'clock in the morning, crying uncontrollably. Mum and Dad were regular bedside companions as I bawled the house down. Both would sit with me and listen as I talked about wanting out and ending my life. I could see no future beyond these four walls. Things were really that bad. I couldn't contemplate a life of depending on others with no hope of improvement to look forward to. In my mind, death was the only way to escape. We would spend hours discussing this and Mum and Dad would persuade me otherwise time after time.

Fran: *We would go over and over the subject and kept telling Hannah, 'OK, what will happen to Jess and Naomi? Who will look after them when we are in prison because you are asking us to do something illegal? None of us would want that, would we Hannah? We'd all want to stick together.'*

I regularly told Mum and Dad to turn visitors away at the door. Even my very closest friends from school were not admitted. As they were now in Sixth Form they had a number of free periods and were prepared to come and see me. For long periods, though, I just didn't want to meet people. Despite me appearing to be impolite and rude, they were really patient with me and I'll never forget that. A district nurse, a friend of Mum and Dad's, came to do my dressing one day and I just didn't want to see her either. I even turned Grandma Ruth away at one point.

I had overcome a long period in intensive care, even longer in hospital, and come out on the other side, admittedly with a difficult future ahead of me. However, I had made it. I was starting to adjust to life as a disabled person only to be dealt another bitter blow and I found that hard to accept. Why me? Hadn't I suffered enough?

I lay inert as days turned into weeks and weeks into months. One part of me wanted to sleep all the time because being awake was really far too torturous. Being awake gave me too much time to think. The only part of my body that I could move was my head and I would often shake it vigorously because it was the only way to get frustration out of my system. By and large, the world passed me by. One specific event that I do remember, though, was the 9/11 tragedy. This was in September 2001 so I had been in bed for about a year. I remember the whole day unfolding in front of my eyes as I watched on TV. Interviews for carers were being held in the front room at the time and I couldn't force myself to join in. I just lay on my bed and watched the Twin Towers come down as terrorist suicide attacks struck the heart of New York.

For a long time I couldn't consider creating a future for myself by trying college or university. The achievement of getting three good GCSEs whilst in hospital seemed a long time ago and as I wasn't prepared to even leave the house the thought of further studying was well beyond me at that point. For months I was just stuck on my bed in Maurice's refurbished garage. I didn't even get as far as the living room.

Getting used to the carers as a constant presence was always going to be tough, but when the days were darkest it became particularly challenging. I was emotionally spent. Feelings and tensions rose to the surface more easily. With at least one carer always on the other side of the bedroom door I was constantly being watched over. Not their fault, I know, but that's how it was.

It might seem strange to detail such a long and significant period in a relatively short chapter, but that is down to me putting the period to the back of my mind and also the fact that there was such monotony about the days. Very little happened to shake off the grim repetitiveness of what I saw and felt.

CHAPTER TWELVE
Emerging from the Darkness

'When I pick out milestone moments this will certainly be one of them.'

Recently, we made an interesting discovery. Mum found loads of letters which had been written to me during that long period in bed. I have had them read to me over and over again and they have made me realise how so many people did so many nice things to support me and my family at that time. The letters are deep and meaningful yet also full of lighter, more trivial issues. My friends cannot resist writing about teenage things like spots and boyfriends! Many mentioned how I was in their prayers and the more cynical side of me would respond, 'Well, the prayers haven't worked.' Mum would reply, 'They have, Hannah, because you're still here.' I had never thought of it that way before.

Finding all the letters and reading them back has been a wonderful experience for me. People forge their own lives and when I became isolated for such a long time it was easy to think that life would move on without me. With the rediscovery of the letters I was deeply touched by the efforts made to think of me and appreciated what had been written in a way that I could not at the time. I showed them to my friends. I also sent my friends a message on Facebook to say a massive 'THANK YOU!'

Susan: *Yes, we used to write letters to Hannah, sometimes in lessons when we should have been working! It was so bizarre reading them quite recently after she had found them again.*

It's funny how small things can trigger off bigger events. One day I had a visit from one of my carers who brought her dog round. Unbelievably, she had walked all the way from Winsford with it. Winsford is a town which lies about six miles south of Hartford so it was quite a trek. She had set off from home on a hot day and finished up at my house. It was no surprise when she didn't want to do it in reverse and asked for a lift home! Her effort that day was to prove significant in aiding my recovery.

The moment I saw her dog I immediately wanted one of my own. When I get the bit between my teeth I don't let go and I kept talking about it long after the carer had left and gone home. Mum and Dad must have been well cheesed off hearing me rambling on and quickly moved to curb my enthusiasm, saying, 'You'd never get off your bed to do anything with it!' They made it very clear that there was no point in me having a dog. The patient who had been stuck on her bed for so long struck a defiant note: 'I'll get off this bed, out of the house and up the road right now if I can have a dog!' This was no idle promise. Mum decided to test me out and asked the Pettys, our next-door neighbours, if I could borrow Rosie, their golden retriever, so that I could take her for a walk. I asked Mum and Naomi to come with me. Mum said, 'What about Dad?' I just did not want it to become like an excursion so I said 'No' to Dad joining the group. I felt really bad about refusing him but, as so often in my life, particularly as a disabled person, I just did not want to draw attention to myself and turn it into a big outing. I think I've improved now. It doesn't worry me so much, as you will see later in the book. Anyway, Mum politely told Dad to back off, which he did. He stayed at home. Sorry, Dad!

The expedition with Rosie took us literally three or four houses down the road. I was then ready to turn back! It was the scariest thing ever, though. I had not heard the sound of cars for almost two years as well as the many other normal, everyday sounds that you take for granted outside. The sky looked enormous and the grass was so green. I was filled with such conflicting emotions, terror yet elation. After that short distance I had had enough and needed to get back to the security of home. We returned Rosie, who presumably was thoroughly dissatisfied after such a short walk, and went back home.

When I look back through my life and pick out milestone moments this will certainly be one of them. Neil Armstrong, the US astronaut, said a classic line in 1969 as he stepped on to the moon's surface, the first human to do so:

'That's one small step for man, one giant leap for mankind.'

It had been like that for me – the shortest of journeys but a huge step forward. I came back saying, 'You'll have to get me a dog now!' Naomi was so excited for me and texted everyone to tell them the news about my momentous trip 'up the road'! It's quite funny, thinking back. A walk covering just a few houses seems nothing, but at the time, it was such a big deal. Our friend Mo was waiting to do my hair when I got back and was amazed at what I had done.

It's definitely true to say that if I had not got poorly, I would never have got Bella. The great day eventually dawned, but I felt awful because I didn't even go and choose my new mate! Mum found a person who had a litter of Labradors for sale, but when she made contact there was only one bitch left. Arrangements were made for the owner to bring the remaining bitch to our house for me to see her. Imagine how excited I was when the tiny, black squirming bundle of fun started licking my face! Bella had come into my life and Dad got a real surprise when he arrived home that evening as she was on my knee. He hadn't expected it to happen so suddenly but by then it was a done deal! He loves Bella now (yes you do, Dad!). The rest of the stuff we needed was in the car boot, which gave Dad another shock when he opened it! Bella slept by my bed and became a real comfort to me.

Celia: When Hannah got her new dog she told me that Bella had chewed her toes and her socks but she couldn't feel it.

Much has been written and said about the pleasure that dogs can bring and there is no doubt that Bella played a big part in my being able to pull myself out of the despondency that had set in. We started to go out for walks to places like Marbury Park on the edge of Northwich, my family pushing me in my manual wheelchair.

I try to walk Bella every day. Jess and Naomi also take her from time to time. Bella knows my moods as well as any human. If I want Mum or Dad and they don't appear she'll go looking for them. Our friend Chris Hynes came for a murder mystery evening and took his characterisation to extremes as he feigned death! Bella always tries to protect me when he comes now, so obviously his dramatic performance on the night impressed one observer!

Bella hates anyone being in my room when she's not there. Sadly, as I write, she is beginning to show her age and her eyesight is not great. I definitely want another dog when she dies. Dad and I went to a disability exhibition at the National Exhibition Centre at the end of May 2012. We were looking at some information regarding assistance dogs. These are specially trained to aid a person with a disability, rather like guide dogs, and it makes sense to think about this option. They are brilliant and are trained to do a lot of basic tasks for you.

Bella isn't the first dog to grace the Rose household. You've already heard about Eric the sausage dog's visit to Alder Hey. While I was in hospital, Dad got a phone call from Martine who was looking after Eric. She asked if he would visit Eric in the vet's. Dad went to the Willows Practice in Hartford where he was told that Eric had spontaneously inflated. The vet wanted to send him (Eric, not Dad) to a specialist in Staffordshire, at a cost of £200 per hour. Dad said 'no' because Eric wasn't insured. He asked the vet if we could just 'pop' him. Eric was like a rugby ball with crinkly skin.

The following day Eric had deflated after a syringe had been put in to draw air out. He had been playing with a stick which had punctured his trachea. When he was breathing the air was coming out of his trachea and into his body. Eric recovered but left the family soon after to go to another owner. Eric had come from a lady who was the seamstress at Mum's school. She had suggested that we might want one of her two dogs because she had two small boys and the dogs were always fighting. When it was obvious that I wasn't going to be home for a while Mum and Dad felt a duty to go back to the lady and ask her what she would suggest we do with him. She understood the circumstances and took Eric back because she thought her daughter in London would be keen to have him.

Eric wasn't the only dog that we decided to move on elsewhere – the other was Romeo the basset hound! I'll let Dad take up this story:

Howie: *Fran was so desperate to get Hannah a dog for when she came home. Rather than go to a reputable breeder she got one out of Loot, the magazine where you can buy, sell or exchange. Romeo lived in the Haydock area and had little resemblance to the character in Shakespeare from whom he took his name! He arrived soon after Hannah got back from hospital.*

Romeo was just the worst behaved dog ever! For a start, he had the loudest, deepest bark and regularly jumped up at you. He found ornaments and chewed them. Romeo even dragged you along when you walked him, he was so strong! We only kept him for a few weeks. The ultimate act was when he was sitting on our lime green carpet begging. He then carried out the act which I will forever remember him for. Romeo dragged himself along the carpet and left skid marks! The previous owners had already said that they were missing their dog [no idea why! Ha!] so Fran rang them back and told them that Romeo could return!

Anyway, back to the story! I improved sufficiently by my 18th birthday in March 2002 to request chicken kebabs! I was getting out of my room by then and came through to the living room to watch television. My fabulous friends came round with a massive card and I thought it was lovely that they had all remembered me. Looking back I think how funny it was that I didn't want to go out on my 18th like any other young person would, but what I did, however mundane, was definitely progress on where I had been over the last 18 months. To show how much further I have moved forward since then, I can definitely say that if my 18th birthday happened now there's no way I would stay at home!

CHAPTER THIRTEEN

Onwards and Upwards

'I found it a real tonic and had a great time.'

As my spirits were improving, I finally got round to thinking about the next stage of my academic studies. I considered the challenge of A-levels. What to do? German was an obvious choice because of my GCSE result. I also fancied doing Law. As with my GCSE I did German with the lovely Jane Copeman. It has always been a subject that I have taken to quite easily and being disabled did not hinder me too much as it wasn't a practical subject like Chemistry. Jane came to my house for a couple of two-hour visits each week although a significant amount of our time was spent gossiping, in English not German! This arrangement lasted for a couple of years, after which I took the exam. I remember 'sitting' it on my bed. It was a really thundery day and I felt poorly. An external examiner came in for my oral.

I spoke about Grandma Ruth coming over from East Germany when her parents wanted to get their children out of the country in 1938 for fear of persecution. It was an amazing story which matches mine for courage against the odds. When arrangements were made to get Grandma and her siblings away to safety, all the visas came through from America apart from hers. One of her sisters also got a visa for England, so the brothers and sisters crossed the Atlantic Ocean while Grandma Ruth came to England on her sister's visa. She was just 17 years old. Grandma couldn't speak English and was put in a kind of boarding house in Manchester. She had to overcome prejudice and language problems. She went to English lessons and met my grandpa's mum who felt sorry for her when she said how much she hated where she was living. An invitation to come to live with them led to Grandma meeting Grandpa and starting a relationship which has stretched to 66 years of marriage.

Ruth never saw her parents again. They both died, one before and the other during the period of the concentration camps. As for her brothers and sisters, she was reunited with them many years later, having travelled across to America to meet up with them. She hadn't been on a plane before so Dad arranged a practice flight to Scotland and back with her and Grandpa. Dad then booked them on a flight out of Manchester. We got to meet the family ourselves because they came over to England. That was really nice!

Grandma Ruth is an inspiring lady who never says much about her past but has confided in me from time to time. I think that it is amazing how she has coped. Like me, she has had to adjust to life from a totally different perspective. Grandma would be very proud of me if she could understand that I was writing my story. Although still alive she is now in a home. Grandpa visits her nearly every day. Jess takes him once a week, as does Dad's cousin. Grandpa also comes to see us on Sundays. Between about three and eight o'clock is our time for family and we look forward to it each week. There are no carers and we can do just what we want, acting like a normal family with the laughter and the bickering! Dad cooks for us, then Jess takes Grandpa back home with an extra portion for his Monday dinner. I love Grandpa and Grandma dearly as well as Grandma Frances, Mum's mum. Grandma Frances is a lovely lady and has a saying which she often uses: 'Hannah, as long as your hands are warm, everything is right with the world.'

As with my GCSE German oral preparation, I had bits of paper all around me to learn and practise from. I remember that we offered the examiner a sandwich. Not many students would have been in that situation during their exams! It was one of many surreal moments over the course of my journey.

There were further positive signs to come. I started to go out more regularly. We went up the M6 to Thornton Cleveleys to visit the Mitchells. While we were there we went along Victoria Road towards the promenade and spent some time on the slot machines. Then I insisted on going down to the beach. I was guided down the walkway on to the sand where the wheelchair began to sink! As we were coping with that problem, it started to rain. We couldn't stop laughing! Mum was anxious to get the van round as she did not want me to get wet, but I had not felt raindrops on my face for 15 long months and wanted to make the most of it. My trousers were soaked but I didn't care! On the way back to the Mitchells, the ventilator fell off the wheelchair. When I got back to their house, Sue tried to dry my wet jeans with her hairdryer without burning my legs. And to complete an eventful day, Bella christened Sue and Dave's carpet by weeing in the hall! *Bella!*

It was, for many, a typical afternoon by the seaside but I found it a real tonic and had a great time. However, this early trip was a sign of things to come as we had to cope with the logistics of getting from A to B to C. Those were the days when I could not do anything without having my ventilator, and preparing me for what seemed a straightforward one-mile walk to the beach was a very time-consuming exercise but something that we knew we were going to have to get used to. We almost needed a team of Sherpas to transport all my necessities, but it was good to get somewhere different, feel the bracing sea air on my face and relive many happy memories of life in Hartford as the Mitchells and the Roses had a good catch-up!

Another massive step was when we went away as a family for a few days late in summer 2002. We were starting to feel more confident about going away and this would be a huge breakthrough. It was both exciting and scary, not least for my parents. The destination was a holiday house with a lovely view over Ambleside in the Lake District. I had always enjoyed family holidays as a child and a few days in the Lake District would have been pretty straightforward back then. Now things were going to get so much more complicated as we planned our short holiday with military precision. Remember those enormous lists you made, Dad?

Howie: *Well, someone had to be organised! You wouldn't want to be coming back home for the ventilator, would you?*

The flexibility in the caring system at that relatively early stage meant that the carers could come with me and they stayed nearby within walking distance.

By now I had a different team leader. Sarah was local, from Hartford, and she was brilliant. She listened to me and encouraged me all the way. We had a really good time and were later to repeat this kind of trip at other destinations. Another one, Worcester, was particularly special because it was the first time that I was able to take my friends with me. We chose a very nice specially adapted cottage taken from a brochure of prestige homes. It felt like I was doing something a bit more normal. Sarah and Lizzy went, along with Mum and Dad, and we paid for the carers to stay in separate accommodation, like at Ambleside.

Back in Ambleside, Sarah arranged for my German result to be faxed through and someone slid the piece of paper under the door of our room. I had passed with a 'B' grade! The place where we stayed gave me a bunch of flowers and when we went out to a restaurant in the evening it was a lovely surprise to see the news announced on the menu: 'Congratulations to Hannah on passing her German A-level!' The whole trip was a huge success and gave us the motivation to plan further trips. Even though our circumstances had changed we now knew that we could get away.

It must have been the Christmas of that year when I went to see Winsford's Christmas lights being turned on. Mum and a couple of carers came with me. Apart from anything else it was a chance to see some celebrities! I'd read there were going to be a couple of characters from Coronation Street and someone from Big Brother.

We couldn't see very well when we got there so one of the stewards told Mum and me to move forward. After a few minutes some women started shouting obscenities at me. 'Get her out of the fucking way,' they were saying. They were speaking as if I was not able to hear them because I was disabled and that upset me. My mum got really cross about it. They were nasty and horrible and it went on for a bit. It was scary and I started crying.

A steward came up and reassured me. 'Don't worry, love, don't worry. Come with me.' He took us round the barriers into this little room behind the shops.

The first person I recognised was Chris Gascoyne, or, more particularly, *Coronation Street*'s Peter Barlow. Sorry if you don't watch 'Corrie', but it was a big deal for me! 'Peter' was there to switch the lights on and immediately saw my red face and that I had been crying. The steward explained to Chris what had happened: 'You wouldn't believe the abuse she has had to take out there.' Chris was really lovely with me. He told me that they were ignorant and to ignore them. Keith Duffy was also there. Keith had been a member of the Irish boy band Boyzone and had joined *Coronation Street* two years after the group had disbanded. He played the part of Ciaran, Peter Barlow's friend, in the soap. Jonny from the *Big Brother* show was also on hand and all three were really nice to me. I was beginning to think that the evening wasn't proving to be so bad after all!

The steward who had brought me in then took me to a special cordoned-off area nearby. The crowd watched as the celebrities turned on the lights before rushing over in my direction to queue for autographs. I soon realised that I was in prime position and already there! I bet my earlier critics were really jealous when they saw me alongside Chris, Keith and Jonny!

Afterwards Mum wrote to the Winsford Guardian to thank the stewards for being so nice to me. The paper rang her back to say that they wanted not only to publish her letter but also to cover the story in a separate article.

Fran: *I told the paper that if it was going to be a disability issue that would raise awareness then we were fine about it.*

The evening had gone from agony to ecstasy and we didn't want to appear to be gloating or making a big deal out of it. Anyway, Alison, one of my carers, turned up a couple of days later for her shift. I will always remember her arrival that morning for two quite different reasons. Unfortunately, our cat had been run over that morning and she was the first to notice and break the news. Alison also had a copy of the Winsford Guardian. The front page headline read 'Nightmare at Switch On' and was accompanied by a picture of me with Jonny. Mum couldn't believe it and I said, 'Oh my goodness, I can't go into Winsford now!' It was funny how Mum hadn't wanted to make a big deal out of it and yet I'd made the front page! I started getting letters and chocolates from Winsford that had been dropped off at the Guardian office. People were saying, 'We're not all as bad as that!'

CHAPTER FOURTEEN

University Challenge

'When the letter was opened I started crying with joy!'

I started Law in the academic year after finishing my German, with Cynthia from Mid-Cheshire College, a further education college with three centres in the area. Cynthia was lovely. I also tried GCSE Biology with Sophie from the same college. I didn't really feel ready to go to the campus yet so, as with Jane, they sent the teachers to me. To be fair to them, I think that they were a bit daunted at first with me on the bed. It wasn't a normal lesson for them by any means. During one of my biology tutorials, Sophie thought it would be a good idea to put some bird seed on top of our white van which stood permanently outside my window. It had been immobile on the drive for the past couple of years as I had been unable to get out during my long illness. It wasn't the most exciting of views from my bed. Grass started to grow and I'm sure that the 'lawn on the van' soon became a fascinating sight to passers-by on Chester Road! It certainly amused me, but despite that, I didn't pursue biology. 'Why am I doing it?' I would regularly think to myself. I wasn't really interested in the subject but felt really bad for Sophie who had been so sweet and lovely company – and I had loved the grass idea!

I covered the Law syllabus over a three-year period because Cynthia thought that was best. I remember doing it on my bed and also in the living room. About a year into the studies, I finally felt able to start going to college. I was extremely apprehensive about it as I had not been in a classroom or around large groups of students since before I was ill. I really wasn't sure how I would cope with the situation.

I also had General Studies course lessons at college with a guy called Mike who was really good. Law was done in evening classes between six and nine o'clock and the carers would come into lessons with me. It must have been an unusual experience for them. Unable to write, of course, I relied heavily on written handouts. I was really nervous at first but got into the swing of things, asking many questions and rediscovering an appetite for learning. It took a while to get to that stage, however, and I felt panicky in the classroom at times. As I have previously explained, I cannot leave a room easily without causing a disturbance. I have never liked drawing attention to myself.

I took my exams at the college, dictating my answers. I was on the ventilator a lot of the time for both lessons and exams. Chunks of information were learnt word for word as I had to rely on my capacity to absorb details.

My studies and examinations completed, I waited for my results. Despite the usual worries about how I had done I had nothing to fear. I secured 'B's in both Law and General Studies, to go with my German result, and was really pleased and proud of myself. The Northwich Guardian returned to record the end of the latest chapter in my academic career!

Onward and upwards! I was on a roll and, spurred on by my success, it was now time to consider university. This was going to be a whole different ball game. My friends were all sorting courses out and it was important to me to be like them. Like them I studied what options were available to me, but inevitably, I had to set my sights differently. They might have had a preference to be far from home or round the corner, but for me, there was no choice. I just could not contemplate studying at distance. Practically, that was out of the question.

> **Lizzy:** *It was hard when we went off to university because most of us went at the same time. When I came home at weekends I remember that my routine was always to make sure that I saw my family, my gran and Hannah.*

I found criminal law fascinating and was also mad on television so when I saw a Film and TV Studies course combined with Crime Studies I had found my two ideal subjects in one package. It was a joint honours degree at Manchester Metropolitan University. The university arranged for me to visit with Mum. I went in my manual chair. The guide was lovely and I thought, 'Yes, I want to do this.'

This period in time, about ten years ago, coincided with a significant change in the administration of the care package. I now came under the auspices of the Complex Care Service, a support mechanism provided through the National Health Service for continuing care beyond hospital. This was intended to give the highest quality of life and independence. It all sounded good in theory but things changed as its influence took hold.

The carers would now 'share' me with other packages, which had not been the case when I first came back home. With so many people coming out of hospital and needing support I might end up having someone in the afternoon who had been with another patient in the morning. There was an increasing amount of red tape and that made things far more frustrating. The administration of everything became much more rigid. There were a host of daily things that carers were now not allowed to do and this kept the onus very much on Mum and Dad to be there and to do those things themselves. Having previously made trips out with a single carer and friends in my van, I now had to have two carers with me at all times. This was hugely frustrating because if there was only one carer around and I had an opportunity to go somewhere it just couldn't happen because of the staffing restriction.

Fran: We were always reasonable and easy-going as a family. We just got on with it because that's the way we are. In 12 years we have met some wonderful carers who have contributed greatly. It's certainly been a learning process both for Complex Care and for us. Hannah did not have control or the ultimate say-so any more. There always had to be a middle person in charge. That was hard to accept. I was criticised for keeping a diary of Hannah's progress, in my own house!

A carer was concerned about things that might be being said about her in Mum's diary, but to me, it was something that Mum needed to keep at an emotional time in our family's life.

> **Fran:** *Some become a little complacent after a while and forget just what Hannah cannot do. It must be like being tied to a chair or a bed for a whole day asking for things. Imagine being like that and the person who comes on duty not even having the decency to say 'Good morning'. There are massive training issues and carers need to realise just what my daughter is up against and what she feels like every day. Getting up and out of bed is difficult enough, but working with people who might not appreciate the problems facing Hannah makes it even harder. I just don't think some people realise.*

Despite the concerns that I've touched on about the new package, there is no doubt that Complex Care helped to get me through university. I was enthusiastic but petrified at the start of the course and a lot of my worries were eased by the help and reassurance given by the carers. I began at the university's Alsager campus about 20 miles south of Hartford and my carers came with me. I didn't feel confident enough alone. I always had to have two carers with me and it must have been deadly dull for them at times, but they supported me wonderfully.

As I have already explained, I can absorb information well, but other aspects of the course posed more problems. I needed people to transfer my thoughts on to paper and prepared some flyers asking for volunteers among the students. Scribing for someone else is a difficult art to perform well but it began to happen and, as a bonus, I made some really good friendships. Aisha scribed loads of my dissertation for me and we are still friends on Facebook, as I am with Louise. Katie and Jenny were also good friends. I really enjoyed the academic challenge and absorbed what was taught in the lessons. Others took notes for me and gave me a copy. Mum helped me read the books at home by turning the pages. That was really frustrating for both of us. I read quickly and kept saying, 'Turn over, turn over!' I covered a lot of ground by reading stuff on the internet. I don't know how I did it, looking back, and wish that I'd kept a diary at the time. I really enjoyed the combination of subjects but, of the two, the criminology had more appeal.

For the media side I had to study films. I watched the 1976 film *Taxi Driver* in Southport Hospital because I was in the ward having surgery on a pressure sore on my bottom. It is a Martin Scorsese thriller set in New York, starring Jodie Foster and Robert de Niro. I remember how bizarre it seemed having to first watch it on the ward then do an assignment about it. Doing essays could be really hard work at times.

The dreaded pressure sore had, indeed, returned to haunt me and I remember that on this particular occasion we tried one of the more grotesque treatments to cure it. Wait for it... maggots were put in my sore to eat away at dead tissue! I was ready to try anything! The staff then used a vacuum machine to suck out dead tissue. Great! I was in Southport for three weeks, which was a nightmare in itself, but that was followed by a further six weeks' bed rest before it healed up.

There were, let's face it, complications all the way throughout my degree course but nothing that we couldn't get round. The teachers were so nice and understanding and I did not have any time off other than when I had my operation on my sore. I don't know how but I completed the course in the normal amount of time.

I really enjoyed university. I was surrounded by people who had not known me before I became ill. This was both enriching and liberating as I had believed that my paralysis would prevent me from ever making new friends again. I met some amusing and wacky characters along the way! I went to socials and invited others back, along with my former school friends, for my 20th birthday in March 2004. It was really nice to have two groups of friends celebrating with me. During the second year it was my 21st birthday and I had a big party. Once again, both school and university life were represented and it meant so much to me on my special occasion.

As I wound up my studies, I really wanted to get a 2:1 degree. Jess and I were doing our degrees at the same time. She was studying Fashion and Textiles in Manchester and a bit of rivalry had developed between us! The tension mounted as we knew that the results would come out within a week of each other. Mine came first.

We all waited at home for the letter to arrive and when it was opened for me I started crying with joy! I had got the 2:1 that I desperately craved. Result! Then Jess got hers a week later, also a 2:1! I completed my hat-trick of newspaper coverage from the Northwich Guardian and really enjoyed my graduation at the Bridgewater Hall in Manchester. Gran and Grandpa joined Mum and Dad for the occasion, as did Naomi and Jess. I went in my manual chair. I couldn't drive my electric chair, which I'll tell you more about later, for the simple reason that with my mortar board on I couldn't have guided it without knocking my 'hat' off! Jess had her ceremony soon after and I was there for her.

I remember someone from the health authority once coming in and saying, 'Have you ever thought of going to university?' and my immediate reaction had been, 'Oh God, I'll never manage that!' Well now I had been to university and I certainly had managed. Along with many thousands of students, my studies were complete. The process through GCSEs, A-levels and university had been made all the more complicated by my condition, but I had come through and was very proud of myself.

Celia: GCSEs, A-levels, university... Hannah's attitude has always been, 'Why shouldn't I do it?' She has never let adversity stop her and I think that's amazing.

CHAPTER FIFTEEN

Looking for a Job

'I was really nervous about going into a new environment.'

There was little time to rest on laurels. The hunt for a job began. Inevitably, my search for work was going to prove more complicated than most. I had a particular fancy to try the media and enquired into various courses at the BBC. Manchester University provided a wide range of opportunities to study aspects of media work so I went a few times. My carers took me and I attended a variety of week-long courses. I began a City and Guild in 'Production' at Mid-Cheshire College and enrolled on a course entitled 'NW Vision and Media' which took me to Granada Studios in Manchester. There was a visit to Cheshire FM radio. I even had a go 'on air' and was told that I had a good voice for radio! They said they would get in touch but I heard no more.

What I really wanted to do was be a researcher. I tried for an apprenticeship at ITV to work on Sir Trevor McDonald's *Tonight* programme, the documentary series which tackled modern issues in a series of half-hour programmes. I did not get anywhere but they gave me some good advice to work on. Every week, meanwhile, my grandpa was asking if there was good news on the job front! I had my fingers in various pies without getting anywhere meaningful. It then became clear to me that I was missing my crime studies.

I did some work with the Citizens Advice Bureau. It was on a voluntary basis and not strictly related to law. I also visited

Northwich Job Centre to see the Disability Advice person, hoping for some options for placements. The lady was very helpful and asked if I fancied seeing a work psychologist. This sounded good. The meeting took place and I told her about my degree and what I had done work-wise so far. I added that I fancied a job with the police. She knew someone at Cheshire Police who was connected with Equality and Diversity. I got in touch with the contact and went to meet a lovely lady called Veronica at Winsford. After getting to know my situation and my aspirations, she asked me what I felt was the best way forward. I said that I'd like to do a placement to get some work experience. Veronica put some feelers out to various departments and one got back. It was a section where they collated data about different crimes. I went to speak to two members of the department. They were so nice and welcoming and asked me if I fancied tackling an issue.

The suggestion was that I do a project on alcohol-related crime in Cheshire. This would be for a couple of days a week on my own for about six weeks. It was 2008 and the first time that I had been in a working environment but the people in the office couldn't have been more helpful. Dad set up the voice recognition program called Dragon Dictate on my computer and showed me how to use a specially-adapted mouse that I moved with my chin.

I was really nervous but soon got into the swing of things and it was brilliant to finally be in the workplace. Soon after starting I heard that there was some more work experience coming up. It was in Human Resources and it was more like the kind of job that I was looking for, less to do with research. The title was Resourcing Assistant and it was a really good opportunity lasting from the beginning of November until the end of December 2008. It was a work trial and unpaid. I really enjoyed it. The next step soon followed and I was offered a further three-month contract in Human Resources. I had now reached the stage where I needed to appoint someone to help me more fully in the workplace. I met Craig from 'Access to Work', an organisation that helped people back into employment, and we interviewed a number of candidates. From that process I met Tia who was to become a big part of my life.

Tia: I had been diagnosed with cervical cancer and had been out of work for some time. It was hard to gain employment as people saw how long I had been out of work. With a degree I was more than qualified and had the experience from before I had been ill but I could not find anything suitable. I was coming to the point where I was banging my head against a brick wall when I received a letter from 'Access to Work' to see if I would go in and talk about getting some employment. They put me in touch with the police at Winsford where an employee called Hannah Rose was looking for a PA. I felt that it was in keeping with my experience and got introduced to Hannah.

Tia and I got on well straight away and it was to be the start of what has developed into a close friendship. After about a month Tia told me that she was moving house. I asked where and she replied, 'I'm going to live on Chester Road in Hartford.' 'I live on Chester Road!' I replied. 'Well, I'm going to be near the Coachman.' 'Oh my God, that's right near my house!' The news just made a perfect working arrangement even better.

Tia: I was between houses at the time and staying in the Northwich Floatel, moored on the River Weaver. In fact, I think I was the very last customer before it closed! A dear friend said that she had a spare room. I'm still there now, three or four years on. It just happened to be that Hannah lived literally a few minutes down the road.

Tia and I were responsible for contacting people who were applying for jobs and dealing with email enquiries. It worked so well that I was offered more work in March 2009. This time it would be a six-month job and I was delighted! People weren't getting full-time jobs anyway.

I was ambitious to develop my career and, although I was enjoying everything that had been put in front of me, I began to start looking at other jobs within the police. My disability was certainly not blunting my motivation. I really wanted to stay with Cheshire Police as they had been so good to me. There were three other positions within the force that caught my eye and applications were submitted. I had an interview each time.

The one for Road Traffic was particularly challenging because the lights went out while I was talking!

A position came up for a vetting officer to check Criminal Records Bureau (CRB) forms. I fancied that, applied and, once again, was granted an interview. Three people met me and I really enjoyed the experience, having benefited from previous interview situations. I waited patiently throughout the afternoon because I knew that there were a number of other candidates. Eventually, one of the three rang me and said, 'Sorry, Hannah, you didn't get the job but you were second.'

I had lost out by two points but was told, 'The person who got the position has done a superb interview and you did well to finish so close.' Although I had come second, I was reassured that in practically any other round of interviews I would have got the job.

It was then explained to me that anyone who comes second for a position automatically gets considered for a job if a further vacancy comes up. Lo and behold, a couple of weeks later, a suitable position became available. I listened to the terms and conditions and was asked, 'Do you want the job?'

I was delighted to accept and couldn't have been happier about how things were going for me professionally. I was in a brilliant place and making new friends. However, not for the first time, a big, ugly barrier was put in front of me just as things were going well. I was stopped in my tracks and my optimism was well and truly dented.

Days after I started the new job I became ill… again.

*First day at school for Naomi
- September 1992*

Hannah and friends at school

Helen and Hannah

A visit from Kate & Anna at Alder Hey

At home with the Mitchells L to R: Susan, David, Kathryn, Gillian, Helen - March 2002

Hannah with Bella - April 2002

Celebrating 18th birthday L to R: (back) Susan, Sarah, Lizzy, Anna, Kate (front) Rosanne, Karen

Birthday celebrations at Millers with Sarah, Lizzy and Anna

With Dr Andrew Selby at my 21st birthday party

Celia, Stephen & Agnes Bentley, with Mo in the middle

Cowboys and Indians!

Face-painting with (L to R) Tia, Limara, Vicki, Naomi, Vicky, Alia & Cat, May 2011

Jess, Naomi and friends from work, August 2011

Michael Owen at the Liverpool training ground

Keith Lemon

Jamie Oliver

The Script's Danny O'Donoghue

Pony ride, Calvert Trust

Abseiling, Calvert Trust

*Ski Taster Day, Bracknell,
September 2008*

First holiday, Lake District, August 2002

Tenerife with Dad, August 2005

Chillin' in Portugal, May 2009   *Naomi & Mum Portugal, June 2010*

With Tia at work

With Naomi, Jess & Bella at Anderton Boat Lift

Mum & Bella at Marbury Park - February 2003

Bostock Singers - Christmas 2008

*Graduation Day with grand-
parents Frances, Lou and Ruth
- July 2006*

Grandpa Lou - January 2012

With my cousins at Grandma Frances' 85th birthday - June 2012

The Rose family - July 2011

With Anne-Marie & Kate, presentation at St John's - July 2012

CHAPTER SIXTEEN
One Step Forward, Two Steps Back
'Yet again, I headed for Leighton Hospital.'

There was a bowling trip planned by work and although I couldn't take part in the activity I was really looking forward to getting to know my new friends and colleagues socially. It was a Sunday evening and my nose had started to run a bit. I did not feel quite right and couldn't go through to the front room for the regular Sunday meal with Grandpa, which was unusual for me.

The next day I was feeling hot and clearly had a temperature. I can only describe my chest as being 'rattly'. A doctor checked me out and told me that I needed to go to hospital straight away. That was absolutely the last thing I wanted to hear. Mum, Dad and one of the carers went with me.

Swine flu had been mentioned as a possibility. This is the common name given to a relatively new strain of influenza which many suffered from in 2009. As it was a new variety people didn't have much immunity to it. It is usually characterised by a high temperature and a number of other symptoms, including a runny nose, so, yet again, I headed for Leighton Hospital. I was beginning to think that I should have my own parking space there! We were ushered into a small room normally used for psychiatric patients. The door was locked and we had to sit there with masks on. Ironically, all my carers had been trained up in how to put a mask on my face but no one had at Leighton. We were shut in that room for about five hours. They wouldn't even let us go to the toilet! I was feeling really poorly by this stage.

Mum and Dad stayed with me after the carer's shift ended and the hospital finally found us a bed.

We went through into another room resembling aliens! Dad was finding the whole episode rather amusing. Typical of his warped sense of humour, he started taking photos. At some times I just don't 'get' Dad and that was certainly one of them!

I was placed in a room on a general medical ward and told that my carers were going to have to look after me because none of the nurses had been trained up in putting protective equipment on. Basically, therefore, there was no point in my being in Leighton when the only people trained to look after me could have done it at home.

It was so hot and there was no fan in the room. There were loads of magazines to look at, but I didn't really feel like reading. I was given Tamiflu, the antiviral drug that was widely prescribed at the height of the swine flu epidemic, but the nurses were still taking care not to come too close. The drug made me feel so nauseous. Mum stayed with me all night and she could see that I was desperate for a fan to get some kind of a breeze going round the room. The hospital said that they didn't have them available any more because of infection control. Mum made it clear that I was burning up. The only place she could think of for getting a fan at that time was the 24-hour ASDA store in Crewe. She went and bought one.

It became increasingly frustrating as we had to stay in the room on our own. A nurse would arrive and talk through the tiniest crack in the door but it was repeatedly explained that they didn't have the training to nurse swine flu so they couldn't come in. As there wasn't a doctor trained to put on the mask and treat the disease, they couldn't prescribe the antibiotics that I obviously needed. I felt like I was a leper.

Dad's mood had changed by now and he was beginning to express his growing frustration: 'This is ridiculous. My daughter's very poorly and she's come to hospital to get some treatment.'

He discovered that he knew the guy who controlled the ward and sent him an email. The ward controller responded by coming to see us only to announce that he hadn't had the training either so couldn't put on the mask or prescribe medicines! By this time, I had been there for 24 hours without the medication that I so obviously needed. To add insult to injury, they had forgotten to turn my special mattress on and I woke up with a pressure sore the following morning. Dad went ballistic.

Lisa, one of my carers, stayed the second night and we watched television together. She was brilliant. By the time I was declared fit enough to go home I still hadn't received any antibiotics. Dad was in Birmingham the day I was discharged. He arranged to pick up the further medicines needed on his way home.

Howie: *I got to Leighton about three o'clock in the afternoon. When I reached the nurses' desk, the sister was on the phone. She chattered away, somewhat anxiously, for about five minutes before putting the phone down. She told me that the prescription had not arrived yet. She said that she had been discussing Hannah on the phone and the result had come back positive. Hannah was the first patient to get swine flu at the hospital. I was told to wait in the patients' day room. I watched some cricket on TV for about half an hour. A doctor came in with the medicines but said that we wouldn't need to take the Tamiflu because it wasn't swine flu! I told him that I'd just been informed that it was!*

Thankfully, all's well that ends well. I had been treated as if I did have swine flu, but it wasn't until it had been confirmed to Dad that I knew for certain – and I was back home by then! Nobody else got it, but I had to be free from visitors for the next four or five days. This meant that I was prevented from seeing my friend Kate who was just back from France, which was so frustrating! Grandad was given a precautionary check because he had been in my vicinity.

I learnt that everybody at the Administration of Justice department at work had got called out of the office into the lobby. The boss told them, 'I don't want to panic anybody but Hannah Rose who started this week might have swine flu.' Apparently, there were a number of gasps to be heard when the news was broken! However, my new workmates quickly recovered their composure and sent me a bouquet of flowers.

I had only been with them for a week! I was really touched that they had organised a collection for me.

Things returned to normality and I went back to work after a frustrating break. I resumed the training that I needed for the new job and found it really interesting. Everyone in my department is lovely and I've made some good friends. I check Criminal Records Bureau forms from all around Cheshire. These outline details about job applicants and help employers throughout the country make safe recruitment decisions. I could be dealing with a teacher or a taxi driver. I'm at the first stage in the process and have to check details closely. If I see something that's relevant I flag it up. There's a massive amount to check and you have to be on the ball all the time. As in every type of work you have targets to meet. Each police force is compared with the others. I do flexi-time, which works well for me. I often think how lucky I am to have such an interesting job. The police in Winsford have been brilliant with me and I will be forever grateful to them.

I'm in a brand new building so all my needs are taken care of. I drive up to my desk and do all my work on a computer through my voice activator; this is fine for one-word and short answers as well as making searches but it's not as accurate and easy when you are trying to write more, as I found when trying to start this book.

I completely rely on computers now, which is funny because I used to hate them. ICT lessons at school filled me with dread! For a start I was really bad at typing and when I worked with a partner we used to swap over so that she did my typing as well as hers, then we'd change back again. Jess was always so much more technical than me.

When I was doing my GCSE English before I got ill I had to do an essay on *Frankenstein* and because I was so rubbish at typing my dad bought me a voice-operated computer program to help me, when I could physically type anyway! Can you believe that? I remember something that my dad said when my illness struck: 'Hannah, you're really going to have to get to know a computer now because it's going to be a massive help to you.' He was so right. It was typical advice from him because he always has to have the latest gadget and loves his computers!

Tia still helps me and corrects things – we work well together and make a good team, don't we, Tia?

Tia: We certainly do, Hannah! I am Hannah's hands and feet on a day-to-day basis. If she needs to complete a worksheet or print some material I'm there to do it for her. I also have to log her on to the computer system each day. I complete the little things that make the working day easier for her. As we got to know each other better we eventually reached the point where I was starting to give her input if she was unsure with the work. I would suggest ways round a problem so that Hannah needn't worry about asking elsewhere if she had done something wrong. This gave her peace of mind. Hannah is just another employee and that's how others see her, on the whole. Sometimes they may ask themselves 'why can't she do that?' but they soon realise why not.

There is no doubting the value put on her at work. Hannah is an inspiration to others and a breath of fresh air every day. I've always been a secretary/PA type of figure so this type of work suits me fine. It's bread and butter stuff but doing it with Hannah gives it so much more meaning. It's also gratifying to me that I have gone from being Hannah's help at work to being part of the team.

Tia walks up to my house in the morning and gets a lift to and from work! How good is that? It is lovely to be alongside someone who I get on so well with as a person.

Tia: I leave the house at quarter to eight and it takes just five minutes to get to Hannah's. I often walk up Chester Road with a smile on my face knowing that Hannah is likely to do or say something that will amuse me! I will then help her get into work. I'll put the bags in the car and get the ramp out. It's worked out really well and I enjoy contributing to her daily routine. She makes me laugh! I love her to bits.

It's really weird how it's all panned out with Tia but perhaps I was owed a bit of good fortune!

Whilst I am working, the carers on duty have time to themselves. There is somewhere separate for them to go to in the building. Some read, others use their laptops. There is a television or they can just watch the world go by! They must always be around when I have my breaks and have their telephones on at all times in case I need to make contact urgently. I get half an hour for lunch. My friends and I all sit together, which is great.

I cannot emphasise too much what brilliant employers I have got. They rallied round when the chips were down and enabled me to take time off when in hospital and are very good at letting me work round appointments. Without exception, they are all people who didn't know me when I was able-bodied so all accept me for who I am. If I make mistakes I expect to be told and that's how I want it to be.

Jessica: Going to work has been the making of Hannah. She has that job because she can do it well. She's able, competent and intelligent.

Since beginning this book I have moved into another part of the vetting office where I now deal with checks for large organisations such as the National Health Service and Social Services. It's really interesting.

CHAPTER SEVENTEEN
Annus Horribilis
'That was just the toughest thing to hear.'

2010 had been a really good year. I was loving work and enjoying the social side. I didn't have any apparent health problems and so I was pushing myself quite hard. I was aiming to get to work by eight in the morning and was often not leaving until five o'clock in the evening so I could build up my flexi-time. I became really obsessive about that and did not realise how much the extra effort was taking out of my body. I just wanted to work and sacrificed many a drinks break during the day to 'clock up the hours'. On Tuesdays I would arrive home and then be straight back out to choir practice.

Choir has been brilliant for me, allowing me to share an experience with some of my closest friends from high school. Having been together in our high school choir, we decided five or six years ago that it would be really good to join another. There was one with a good reputation at Sir John Deane's College in Northwich but it was fully booked. We decided to join another, called the Pyramid of Sound, in Warrington. Alison, one of my carers, offered to drive me and my friends. We liked it and made some good friends but it wasn't our kind of thing and we wanted something a bit more challenging and professional to match what we had been used to at St Nicholas High School.

Places then came up at Sir John Deane's and we moved. We loved it so much and it helped being so much closer to home, just a couple of miles away. Family friends Colin and Sheila were in that choir as well. We did some really good songs and it was a massive thing to me because it was something that I could do with my friends on an equal basis. I was able to raise my electric wheelchair when the choir stood up to sing, which made me more able to take part.

The choir leader, Ally, then decided to have a break and someone else took over. It didn't quite suit us as well but we then found that Ally was setting up another choir. We moved with her and became known as the Bostock Singers. The new venue was even more convenient as Hartford Methodist Church was just down the road.

We are still there and rehearse every Tuesday evening. We do fun songs and concerts and even get paid to do events! We are really good, even though I say it myself!

Lizzy: I joined the school choir in Year 9 and saw more of Hannah because of that. We loved choir so much at school. Even when there are other things happening I always make the effort to go to choir practices now because it's a social thing as well, not like at school when there was so much seriousness around it. This is totally the opposite. You go along and sing for pleasure. You relax and don't worry about anything else while you are there. My sister, Jenny, goes as well. It's also helped Hannah with her breathing and she's got so much stronger because of it.

Sarah: *The choir has been very important to Hannah, from school right through her life. Through it, she has established her core group of friends. Singing has given her so much more as well. I've heard of reports of the physical and psychological benefits provided by singing. It's used in workplaces for team-building and is supposed to be good for mental health and physiologically.*

Choir is always one of the things that I miss most when I'm ill but, fingers crossed, I'm back now and enjoying it! I have made some really nice friends through it. Everyone is so kind. I had to leave early at a Christmas concert once because I didn't feel well. It was so embarrassing. Everyone was ringing me afterwards to see if I was all right.

I love singing but, as well as that, it is a chance to socialise. At this point in my life it was something that I looked forward to every week and I never minded heading off out after a day at work. So, all was going well for me. Typically, it was not to last.

On New Year's Eve, as my positive year drew to a close, I was told that I had a red patch on my bottom. We always kept a close eye on my skin because I was constantly worried about it. It didn't look like a pressure mark so I carried on. Within a week, though, the area started to look noticeably angrier. I was enjoying a two-week Christmas break and was due to go back into work on 10 January 2011.

The mark grew ever more distinct, but having had my time off work for the festive season, I was doubly determined to go back to my desk and get into the routine again. I did just that, reporting for duty at Winsford on the scheduled day.

Tia: *Hannah is paranoid when she isn't at work through illness or injury. She worries about her job being on the line when times are difficult in the workplace, but I reassure her that she cannot be blamed. She has never bunked off. I keep telling her how much she is valued and that her work is excellent.*

Just two days later, one of my carers told me that things had got worse and that I should not go in to work that day. We sent for the district nurse, who decided that I would be fine to get up out of bed. I was moved to an armchair where I could adopt a different position and take pressure off the troublesome area.

Everything then went rapidly downhill from January to the middle of March as the sore became more acute. It affected me physically and mentally and, yet again, I returned to the darker days. Whoever was out there controlling my destiny was bent on inflicting maximum torture. Why does one person have to suffer so much misery? What had I done to deserve all this? The questions I asked myself were endless. It pained me to think that I had overcome all the odds to settle in at a lovely workplace where I didn't expect any special dispensations and here I was, having to take time off yet again.

Lizzy: *It was a really bad setback because of the way in which Hannah had become much more independent. She had progressed at work and it was like she was back at square* *one and everything that she had achieved had suddenly been whipped away from her. The hardest thing was seeing someone you care for so upset but not being able to do anything at all to help.*

My 27th birthday arrived and my friends came round to see me. I was still using the armchair with movement back and forward from the living room to the bedroom. I thought that the sore was improving bit by bit until one of the district nurses came out to apply the dressing. She said there was something not right because she had noticed weeping from the sore area. We thought it was all part of my recovery process so the routine continued. It was not long before we discovered that our quiet optimism was to be shattered. A further district nurse visit revealed that there was a massive hole some seven centimetres deep in my bottom.

On reflection we should have consulted the experts at Southport Spinal Injuries Unit earlier. They may not tell you what you want to hear, but they know what they are talking about. Now we knew we had to get in touch and went over on April 3. I went by ambulance because they didn't want me to sit up on my sore.

The medical team at Southport told us that if I hadn't come in that day, the hole was so close to the bone it could have poisoned my blood. This totally blew apart our notion that it was healing. Dad was upset that we hadn't reacted quicker, but Mum told him that we couldn't think like that. I was told that the situation required total bed rest and that was just the toughest thing to hear. I was screaming, 'Just kill me now, I'd rather be dead'. I was overwhelmed with grief once again and I cried all the way home. I told Mum that the only way I was going to cope was by moving my bed into the living room. I couldn't face being in my garage bedroom again for the coming weeks. It took me back to my post-GCSE days and that awful two-year spell.

It was a Thursday and I was so determined to get what I wanted that I rang the bed people straight away to get them to move my bed. I was told that they could not do anything until the Monday and that absolutely freaked me out. The district nurse came out and I told her straight away that I would rather be dead. She suggested that I get some candles to put round the room and make it cosy and calm which was really sweet of her!

I remember that first weekend so well. It was hot and sunny and I've always been one for feeling my best when the sun is shining. I was desperate to be outside. My dad's like that as well. We hate being stuck inside on days like that.

Kate: Hannah's always been a sun lover. She would get a good tan which always made us jealous!

All I remember saying to people was, 'It's only April, it's only April so things can't be this nice for long, can they?' Well, the weather was. In fact, the weekend proved to be boiling hot and I was stuck in my bedroom with the door shut! Those two days were the worst ever and my friend Lizzy gave up her whole Sunday with her sister, Jenny, to watch DVDs with me. The company of the two of them got me through the weekend because I was in a really horrible place emotionally.

Lizzy: Hannah was very upset and we went over straight away. She was on her bed in her room and she kept saying, 'I hate it, I hate it'. We took a film just to try and distract her. All you can say to Hannah is, 'It's going to be all right,' but you know it's not. You find yourself saying something like, 'It'll be just two more weeks'. It's so difficult when you know you cannot do anything to help her. Being there is the only positive thing that you can do. Hannah is so inspiring and I talk about her a lot in my lessons at school in health- and care-related issues. The children cannot believe that she can do all she can do when she is disabled.

Kathryn: We had to do a presentation at school – it must have been around the time of GCSEs – about someone who had inspired us. I chose Hannah and everyone was crying. I got a distinction for it. We also did a sponsored activity and raised over £300.

I told Mum and Dad that there was no way that they could go out into the sunshine when I couldn't. The bed people eventually arrived and while they moved my bed from one room to the other via the narrow kitchen in our house I used my final 20 minutes of freedom to sit in a chair in the garden. I soaked up my last rays of sunshine for three months. I was to be stuck in my bed until July.

Nurses visited every day to measure the wound and I would ask them constantly if there was progress. 'Is it healing?' I enquired hopefully. I was very poorly at times and kept getting awful headaches. Until then I had rarely burdened my friends with my inner feelings. This was different and I released my emotions on many occasions.

> **Celia:** *Hannah often hid behind a very good mask, not showing her true self to visitors during her dark days. I had been like that as well when I was recovering from my brain tumour. I was pleased when she showed how she really felt and that she didn't think that she had to put on a front for us.*

Another great support during those dark days was Sarah. Sarah is an incredible person. As well as always being there for me as a friend she is also a PA for her two brothers in Leftwich, a village just south of Northwich. The brothers share a similar condition and are in wheelchairs. I suppose this is one particular reason why I've grown closer to Sarah since I got ill. She and her family have helped a lot because they've had to deal with disability as well. When they started advertising for personal assistants they asked me to be on the interview panel. It was a really good experience for me and helped when I started with mine. Since then, Sarah has helped interview for my positions. We each have experience that can benefit the other.

> **Sarah:** *The bulk of our friendship has been since Hannah became disabled, but I don't separate things into before and after. We've shared in each other's dark days. I've lived around the world of disability all my life. I've always known people in wheelchairs and people with support needs. My brothers' disabilities present quite a different situation from Hannah's. They were born with*

it, have learning difficulties and no speech. There is, however, a lot in common between the two families – the impact, for instance, of having people in your home who are paid to care and the effect on the family dynamics. There's a lot which we can share and understand that will benefit and strengthen our friendship. I guess there are things we can say to each other that we wouldn't share with anyone else.

Hannah and I are also the only two of the group still in the Northwich area. Sometimes we will just allow ourselves a night where we let ourselves go. Storing everything up isn't good. A takeaway and a good natter help us to unwind. Hannah's progressed in a million ways. We all grow in confidence as we get older. We all do things that we haven't previously. The things that have happened to Hannah have gone hand in hand with her growing maturity. She's just had more obstacles put in her way than most.

One evening during this awful period Sarah and Lizzy had promised that they would pop in after choir practice and, unbeknown to me, they brought the whole choir with them! I got the shock of my life when they came into my room followed by all the other members. It made me cry. Afterwards I began to realise why Mum had told me to take my duvet off as I looked a mess and why she was vacuuming my room. It had puzzled me at the time. I just couldn't understand the effort she was making for my two friends. The neighbours stood outside listening.

Lizzy: *Hannah rang me around my birthday time to say that she couldn't come to my party. She was really sorry. We asked around at choir if anyone fancied cheering her up by going to sing to her. There was a good response. Quite a number know the family and others knew Hannah and we got over 20 to come along.*

It was a horrendous time for me and the efforts made by such close and loyal friends were appreciated. Alison, my carer from the start, sat on my bed as I told her, 'Alison, I can't go through any more. I just can't do it'. She said, 'Hannah, in all the time I've been here you've had low points and you've come back stronger every time. I'm not worried about you because you will do that again. I know you too well!' They were kind and inspiring words which did their bit to help get me through. Alison is one of the loveliest people I know. She has been with me so long that she has seen Jess and Naomi go all the way through high school and university into employment and I've seen her children grow up as well.

Others played their part and helped to ease the pain by going out of their way to say and do nice things. One very special friend was Andy.

I had first met Andy a couple of years earlier. Andy was an able-bodied young man who went to Goa on holiday with his friends about six years ago. He walked into the sea until it was waist-height, waited for a wave and then dived into it, head-first. It's the kind of impulsive move that people make on holiday countless times every day of the year. Andy hit something hard, probably a rock, and his friends looked across in horror as he lay, face down, in the water. He was in agony and unable to move. He had broken his neck.

Andy's friends dragged him clear of the water. Another holidaymaker, who was a British medic, secured his neck with two large Coca-Cola bottles and used a restaurant's chalkboard as a stretcher. They all carried him up the shore and into a van and rushed him to hospital. In intensive care, doctors discovered he had broken his neck in three places and had crushed his spinal cord.

Andy: *The hospital was so basic, like a scene out of MASH. There were people dying left, right and centre, and I could feel the doctors drilling into my skull.*

After four days Andy was transferred to a specialist hospital in Delhi. His family flew out to join him and were told he was unlikely to survive – and if he did, he would probably be brain-damaged.

Andy: *I could have given up at that point, but I was really determined. I wasn't even thinking of the fact that I was paralysed. I just wanted to live.*

For six weeks, Andy was on a ventilator and unable to speak. After two months he was transferred to a hospital in Britain where he spent a further eight months. He never lost his sense of humour.

Andy: *My family thought those six weeks where I couldn't speak were the greatest blessing. I've always had a sense of humour about it. Even when they were rushing me to hospital I was joking about the Coca-Cola bottles, and not a day went by in Delhi where we didn't find something to laugh about. I remember Mum crying at my bedside and me saying, 'Mum, I promise you, I'll make something good out of this'.*

Until then, Andy had been leading a normal life like me and now he had no option but to adjust to life as a tetraplegic, paralysed from the shoulders down. He was gutted that he had been at a lovely part of his life and it had come to an end. He admitted that he said goodbye to many things at that moment.

Andy lives in Oldham and you may know of him from a storyline in the television soap *Emmerdale*. His TV character, Steve Kelly, was involved in one of the programme's most controversial storylines, which featured the assisted suicide of Jackson Walsh. Andy's character joined the show in February 2011 as Jackson's friend and tried to persuade him that being paralysed need not be a negative thing following an accident in the show when his out-of-control van was hit by a train.

I was having physiotherapy when I first met Andy. I had gone to see a different therapist in Bury. The therapist said that a friend of hers had had an accident and she thought that he might benefit from meeting me. I rang him and he came to visit with his girlfriend. He was such a laugh and we got on so well. Andy's also a mad keen City fan.

It is no exaggeration to say that my lovely friend Andy was thinking about me every day during that awful period in 2011. I knew that for sure because he contacted me every day, perhaps a phone call or otherwise a text, and it meant so much to me. I'd hear his strong northern accent coming down the phone. If my friends were with me, he'd shout, 'You all right, girls?' Andy wants what I've got in terms of a care package, but they aren't available in his area yet. He has agency nurses and they live in with him because he was in his own home at the time of his accident. Andy also has an iPhone which he uses through his wheelchair. I really need one of those, then I can ring people and they can ring me when I want and it's more personal.

Andy was brilliant and his support helped me during that very difficult period which lasted weeks and months. It must have been unbearable for my family.

Jessica: There was just no let-up, no light at the end of the tunnel. Many a time we sat with Hannah and she shared her darkest thoughts with us. I would try to lift her spirits, but it was so hard. She just did not want to go on. She wanted us to help her die. It got to the point where I said, 'Hannah, this is your life. If you really want to go that way there will be means and ways of doing it.' Then I would resort to saying things like, 'Don't you want to know what happens on this storyline in Hollyoaks *before you go?' We gave her mundane examples like that to help make her think that life was worth living for and that she should go on for a bit longer. I'm not saying that it was just* Hollyoaks, *the TV programme, that made the difference, but it certainly helped!*

Jess is not exaggerating. I was really desperate. I pleaded with my mum and dad to help me end my life. They would always say things like, 'Hannah, if a cure came along, how would we then feel?' Mum and Dad knew I would never go through with my intentions, but there were definitely times when I seriously questioned whether I could cope.

Jessica: I remember being out for a walk much later with Hannah and Bella. It was a lovely day. I said to her, 'Hannah, think of this moment now and then think back to when you were flat out on your bed saying you couldn't continue. If you'd known then that times like these were ahead would you still have been saying, "I don't want to be here"?'

The fact is that I wouldn't. I hate to admit it, but my sister's right!

One of the events that I had to miss during this awful time was my friend Jenny's wedding but all was well in the end because she and her husband arranged to get 'married' again, this time at my house after I had recovered. A lot of organisation went into it and Dad arranged a Jewish wedding, even though they are not Jewish! He even 'conducted' the service. Jenny came in her wedding dress and Julian, her husband, in his tuxedo. We had bridesmaids as well. It was amazing and I filmed it all on my BlackBerry. Jenny is expecting now, but somehow, I don't think that they will be recreating the birth for me in my living room!

With spring moving into summer on the other side of the window, my spirits started to lift and I went to great lengths to get my fix of sunshine. I asked, 'What's the difference between being on a bed outside and inside?' I was told that the transferring process was difficult and that I could not go in a hoist. However, we found a way of giving me a temporary reprieve.

Mum and Dad bought a camp bed from Argos and, with my carers' help, managed to get me out into the garden. I was moved off my bed, which I shouldn't have been, but I think that sometimes you have to take some risks in life. Even my dad, who's the biggest worrier ever, said, 'Come on, let's do it!' I made it into my chair and was quickly pushed out, down the ramp and into the garden. The carers took the hoist from my bedroom and pushed that down as well. Then they took the mattress off the bed and took it outside, placing it on the camp bed. It was typical of the military-style operations to which I had become accustomed but it succeeded and having the sun on my face again was the best feeling ever! Some of the carers felt that we shouldn't be doing it, but what the heck! I had a parasol to shield me from the bright light and a fan on and I was boiling, but I just didn't care because it was a change of scenery and it was lovely!

On the way back into the house one day Naomi was pushing me up the ramp. She needed to tip me back a bit to negotiate the slope. Suddenly, I started falling backwards. Naomi managed to 'catch' my head, which was fortunate because I would have hit concrete, but gravity took over and everything else fell back. Pat was the carer on duty inside the house. She opened the door, little expecting what she would see outside. Wheelchair lying at an angle, me flat out, Naomi cradling my head! We had to get the hoist from my bedroom. Fortunately, my sling was underneath me so we just needed to hook it on.

There was another occasion, probably about four years ago, when I was sunbathing in the garden with my legs up. I wanted to readjust my position to stay in the sun, got it completely wrong and reversed into a flower bed! I shouldn't have driven the chair with my legs up but paid the price. It was like slow motion as the whole chair flopped onto its side. Fortunately, my head hit the soft soil, but I lay there for about five minutes not knowing what to do. Obviously, I couldn't feel anything with my body but emotionally my mind was in turmoil! Why? Martine was having a barbecue party next door and I was praying that no one would wander down the garden at that point. Can you just imagine what they would think as they casually glanced over the fence? A Rose lying in the roses! I hate fuss and was just praying that this wouldn't happen. To make things worse, my trousers were quite far down my bottom and the carers were inside the house! I didn't want to risk drawing attention to myself by shouting for one. I didn't know whether to laugh or cry!

Eventually Pat (yet again!) and Karen came out. They had to unstrap the chair from me, lift it up and then hoist me off the floor. I was hysterical with laughter by now, knowing that help was at hand. Dad was at the Thundersprint, an annual motorbike festival in Northwich, which was probably just as well because I think he'd have had the biggest heart attack ever if he'd seen me. I went through the full details when he returned, with the help of the odd porky! The left armrest had bent where it landed on the ground and I told him that I'd driven over a basketball! All he could think to say was, 'Is your chair OK?'

I was so lucky not to hurt myself. As you can imagine, the electric wheelchair took a lot of getting used to and I did loads of damage along the way including twice fracturing bones in my leg. About five years ago I was getting out of the van at university and turned round. My carer started lifting the tailgate before I had spun round sufficiently. I drove my wheelchair to one side, but my foot stopped where it was. I broke my tibula and fibula. We rang my mum and dad and they could not believe what had happened. We met up at Leighton Hospital (again!) and I had to have a cast up to my thigh. On a later occasion I needed a chest X-ray before going on holiday to Portugal. I did not realise that the wheelchair was switched on, leant backwards, activated the control behind my head and flew across the room, breaking my ankle! I have learnt from painful experience and the wheelchair has become far easier to control and, undoubtedly, allows me to do much more for myself.

The physical understanding of how to operate the wheelchair is one thing, but there is also a mental side to overcome which is arguably even greater. I developed a strong resistance to using an electric wheelchair at first because I thought that it made me look more obviously disabled. The advantage of the manual one where I was pushed along by somebody else was that it made me look as if I had had an accident and would eventually recover. This was how I wanted to play it. I don't think it was about not accepting my condition because I don't think I ever will. It's just that I didn't want to look like I was disabled. It was an attempt to convince people that my indisposition was temporary and that I would be back on my feet one day even though, in my heart, I knew that it was not going to happen. It was a sign of the vulnerable and insecure side of me that has been present throughout my life.

It took me about two years to pluck up courage to use the more advanced electric model. Looking back, I can't believe that the electric chair sat gathering dust for all that time because I can't do without it now. It is a sign of how much I have progressed mentally over the years that I have cast off my insecurities and embraced the technology. I will happily stop the machine on my dog walks and engage passers-by in conversation without worrying about the need to convince them that I haven't always been like this.

My electric wheelchair has given me a new 'freedom', but back in the garden on that comical afternoon when I landed in the flower bed, I was left feeling a bit scared now that I knew the chair could tip over. When I'm walking Bella I sometimes worry about going over rough ground. Dad might tell me to hurry up, but I don't want to push things. It just affects your confidence a little bit.

My friends from work formed a Tuesday club when they would come to see me at home. One of the things we did was watch home videos. They would say, 'Oh, my God, Hannah! You're walking on these videos!' I wanted them to know that I haven't always been like this. I never thought I would find another group of people that I loved being around as much as my school friends, but I have become very close to my friends from work. They don't treat me any differently. I didn't want them to think of me as 'Hannah in a wheelchair' and they don't. I also think that it has meant a lot to Jess and Naomi to see me making new friends.

Here's another example of how lovely they are. Vicky, one of my work friends, organised someone to come and do some face painting at Tuesday club and I had a make-over. She took my picture afterwards and, lo and behold, it appeared on a surprise birthday cake. Brilliant!

As July came to a close, things began to pick up more. The sore began to close up and mend. I could feel real progress at last. It was a wonderful day in August when I went back to work on a phased return. My work have had to put up with so much over the years and my boss was so concerned that I did not rush back too quickly that he told me to start with an hour. I said, 'An hour! I can't work for just an hour!' I had to be retrained as I had forgotten everything. I'd not worked for seven months, you see. However, piece by piece the jigsaw was completed and eventually I was back in the swing of things.

A little while later I took my next few days off. It was October half term and Mum and I had a chance to spend some time together as she wasn't in school. We talked about hitting the shops and making family visits, but above all, it meant some quality time with each other and I felt well enough leading up to the break to want to make the most of it.

I had got myself back on track, but yet again, things did not go according to plan as I was to experience yet another setback in the ebb and flow of my life.

CHAPTER EIGHTEEN

Back in Hospital

'I just felt like a useless, dead weight.'

Mum and I went shopping in Chester. Retail therapy still remains a treat and I have also developed a dreadful habit of ordering things online! I can do it myself now as I can activate my own security code through a keyboard on my computer, which is dangerous. It was very liberating at first, but like many others, I started spending money I didn't even have!

I was getting really bad headaches during the half-term holiday and, at times, it felt as if my head was about to explode. We had reached Primark on Foregate Street in Chester. I sat inside the shop saying to myself, 'Oh my God, my head, my head...' The pain was beginning to travel down my neck as well. Mum wanted us to go home but I said no, and then the headache suddenly eased. However, as a precaution, we rang the hospital in Southport and explained everything that we thought they needed to know, including the fact that I had a big blister on my toe. They said that the blister could be triggering the pain and suggested we come in for a check-up.

Autonomic dysreflexia had returned to haunt me. If you remember it had first struck just after I got my GCSE results. When an irritating stimulus is introduced to the body below the level of the spinal cord injury, like the blister on my toe, nerve impulses are sent to the spinal cord where they travel upward towards the brain. They are blocked at the injury and the consequence is that my blood pressure is raised and that is the dangerous part of the condition. Medication was needed once again. Luckily we carried the medicine with us. However,

Southport Spinal Injuries Unit wanted to double-check my condition and run a few tests so I arranged to visit the following day.

I didn't take anything with me apart from essentials because I thought that I was just going to be visiting as an out-patient. Ha! Little did I know! The hospital gave me a bladder X-ray because it was common for the bladder to be a cause of the headaches felt in autonomic dysreflexia. I was lying on the table when Eddie, who does the X-rays, asked, 'Have you had a scan done lately, Hannah?' I replied, 'No,' and from his reaction I could sense that something wasn't quite right. He walked out of the room.

As I left the room, Mum said, 'Hannah, you're not going to believe this!' I was moved over to the X-ray picture and it was like one of those joke skeleton cartoons that you see on the television. There, clear as daylight, was a stone in my bladder and it was the size of an apple! Normally, they are up to 2 cm in diameter. They had found the cause of the pain. Anything that causes urine to stagnate in the bladder creates the potential for stones to form because waste products won't be removed as normal. I had had problems with various stones on occasion but these had been minor. On this occasion, they would have to cut me open because of the size of the beast. On reflection, it was a good job that they asked me to come in because we would have carried on thinking the blister was the root of the problem.

However, that was not on my mind at the time. When I was told that I would have to stay in hospital for a minimum of two weeks, I was distraught. I had avoided going to hospital for so long with my pressure sore. Living at home during that terrible time earlier in the year had made me feel relatively happier, but now I was facing another period in hospital and it was a bitter pill to swallow.

The problems through 2011 and this latest setback were so hard to bear and I kept saying to myself, 'Come on, give me a break, *I don't deserve this*.' I had already been booked into theatre at ten o'clock the following morning and had been allocated a hospital bed, which is normally so difficult to get in Southport General Spinal Injuries Unit.

I was clearly unprepared. I didn't have my ventilator with me; I had none of my stuff, in fact. The nurses got me on to my bed, where I had to wait while Mum drove back home and returned with what was needed.

Mum and Dad took time off work for the operation the next day. As soon as I came round the staff showed me the stone. In fact, they put it right in front of my face! They were clearly impressed by its size. 'The biggest we've seen in 15 years!' was what they were saying. Back in the ward my dad then made Mum hold it while he took a picture on his BlackBerry, which didn't impress Jess and Naomi! I half expected it to finish up on Facebook and Twitter and, while we're at it, why not sell it on eBay? That was on the Friday at the end of half term. I clearly wasn't myself over the weekend. I remember watching Strictly Come Dancing on Saturday and crying. Brucie and Tess didn't usually get to me that way!

Television has always been a comfort to me. I've found that the only way through a dark period is to escape and that is what I am able to do by watching television. Everyone jokes about the amount of TV I watch, but through it, I can let other thoughts and stimuli take over my mind rather than my own.

My 'Possum' enables me to put that into practice without physical help. 'Possum' means 'I can' in Latin and the technology is designed to provide independence for disabled and elderly people. Suddenly, it is possible to do a variety of everyday tasks that others would take for granted. The Possum has a screen and a menu and I can scroll through the menu by sucking on the attached tube, allowing the cursor to move to where I want it to be. It allows me to watch what I want on television, record it, play it back, change the volume and watch DVDs. As well as enabling me to control how I watch television, the system lets me operate the lights and the sound system at home. It can also produce a noise which brings someone in if I need help.

Being in Southport felt very strange. I was in an open ward where there were others who had recently suffered their own spinal injuries. They were not in a good place physically or mentally, worried and depressed about what the future held for them. There was too much time to think. It reminded me all too clearly of my own time in Alder Hey.

I really did not feel myself and needed my mum and dad constantly. I wanted to go home so much. Dad brought Grandpa,

Jess and Naomi on the Sunday and all the time I was repeating, 'I want to go home.' Jess said I couldn't and that I had no option. It was a typical reaction from her. She is so much like my dad in character – straight down the line. Perhaps that's what you need at times like that. I cried constantly and felt awful. Monday was the worst day of all because Mum and Dad were back at work and I was on my own with the nurses. They were lovely but I felt so low as all my nearest and dearest would be back in their own weekly routines. If you imagined my journey through my whole illness on a line graph, this part would be right at the bottom. It was horrible.

Suddenly and spontaneously, I asked for my phone. I was feeling upset, crying and needed to ring Mum. I just wanted to hear her voice. This showed how I wasn't thinking straight. Firstly, you are not allowed to use your mobiles on the ward and, secondly, I would never normally put that much pressure on my mum who would, no doubt, have her own work commitments to deal with at school. However, I persuaded someone on the ward to ring her school number. The tears were rolling down my cheeks as I heard the dialling tone at the other end. After several seconds, the school secretary answered. I was bawling my eyes out by now and pleaded with her, 'Can you get me Fran Rose, please? I'm Hannah, her daughter.'

The secretary hesitated momentarily and replied, 'Sorry, I don't know where she is.'

'But I really, really need her,' I cried down the phone. I was not going to take 'no' for an answer.

I was still crying when I finally heard Mum's voice in my ear. She was in tears as well. Momentarily, I forgot my own emotions and asked her what was wrong.

It was the day that Mum had gone back after half term and she had learnt that a pupil had died. I had rung wanting her attention so much, only to realise that she also had to be at school to comfort her 'other family'. Poor Mum. She must have been under massive stress with me, then with the news of the unfortunate child and the effect on the others in the class. I felt so selfish. It was one of those moments when I fully realised how much strain I was putting her under.

I have to say, the nurses at Southport were really good. They calmed me down and tried to raise my spirits by using me as an inspiration to others in the ward: 'It's really good that you're here, for others to see that you've been home and that you are now working. It will be such a boost for them.'

That was nice of them to say, but nevertheless, I felt trapped and it took me back to when I had spent long periods on my bed at home. I revisited experiences that I had known before and never wanted to have again. There had been so many positive things happening in my life, academically, job-wise and socially, but now it was as if I had taken a massive step backwards again. I felt strapped to my bed, tied down, and the fact that I was never going to be able to move was a constant gnawing feeling inside me again. It would scare me that I couldn't do anything. I just felt like a useless, dead weight. I experienced pins-and-needles-type tingling sensations and was desperate to move to sort them out but could not. These feelings of utter negativity come to the surface when I have prolonged periods in bed. They don't affect me as much when I am busy, which is why work and why friendships are so important to me.

My brilliant friends came on the Monday night, dressed in Halloween outfits with some little goodies to cheer me up, but I just cried. Mum decided to give us some space which allowed me to have a really good chat with them.

Lizzy: *When you see people in their most difficult times and you are sharing something big and important it makes the friendship stronger because you are together on a journey.*

Tuesday was also really bad and I continued to be upset. I was so desperate to have someone with me that I paid two of my support team to come and keep me company. Looking back, I feel guilty about not telling others that I was there and Maurice went mad when he found out! The pair stayed till about half past four and that was so good. It was lovely to have familiar faces to help me. From then on I didn't have a day when there wasn't someone there with me.

They were testing times and I felt really vulnerable as if I couldn't cope with anything. I went to see a psychologist. I had seen one previously and he wasn't terribly helpful. This time my emotions came out. He said, 'Hannah, what you are going through is totally normal. We've done lots of studies about how people cope when going home and then coming back into hospital.'

I replied, 'I think I'm going crazy, cracking up.' Then when I realised that I was going to have to go back in early 2012 after Christmas for a further monitoring visit I felt even worse. I was saying, 'I can't enjoy Christmas, I can't enjoy anything,' because I had this return visit hanging over me. However, I had an important ally. Susan and Celia's dad, Stephen Bentley, came with me on my next visit to Southport to lend support as an experienced consultant.

To make matters worse, the doctors had found another stone at around the same time they found the jumbo-sized one in my bladder. This time it was in my kidney. Kidney stones are hard crystallised deposits that form in the kidneys and become lodged in the urinary tract. Larger ones can be really painful and hard to pass through the system so sound waves are passed into the body; the waves are supposed to blast the stones into smaller fragments so that they can pass out more easily.

I had a kidney function test towards the end of 2011 and went back for the results in January 2012. If the kidney had not been functioning they would have had to take it out, but they decided they would try to 'blast' the stone out over a few visits, which was the better option. Despite this, there was still plenty for me to worry about. I had numerous plans already in place over the next few weeks and months and hoped that hospital visits wouldn't get in the way. There were to be four blasts in all and each would have to be followed by a minimum of three weeks before the next. There was also the recurring issue of inconveniencing my work with more time off, although I knew they would understand. They always did.

I must have driven the staff mad with my conflicting emotions, but on a positive note, I made some good friendships with the nurses. The thought that I didn't know when I was going home was a nightmare and returning to work seemed a long way away. I was at Southport for three weeks in all and went back to work a week or so after leaving hospital, albeit on a phased return – once again. I started again knowing that there might not be much continuity over the coming months because of the return visits to deal with the kidney stone, and it was so frustrating.

It was particularly shocking because I had honestly not expected to be going in for anything more than an initial check as an out-patient. What had started as a shopping trip in Chester with Mum had turned into a nightmare. I was getting used to having to expect the unexpected. The experience reinforced again how important and supportive my family was to me. I really needed my mum and dad when I went to Southport and felt like a child again, reliant on support.

The original bladder stone is still in my bathroom at home. I bet it stinks now! When I got home from having it out in hospital, my friends wanted to see it, but Mum insisted they stay outside and look at it through the window because it smelt so bad!

CHAPTER NINETEEN

A Big Step in the Right Direction

'I am now in control of my destiny.'

I said goodbye to the horrible 2011 and, despite my knowing that there would be ongoing disruption and worry with the kidney stone, fortunes began to turn for the better in 2012.

Instrumental in this upturn were major developments for the better in my system of support. These had started to take effect towards the end of 2011 and the two ladies who visited me in Southport were part of my new team as we moved to personalised health budgets.

After years dominated by the rigid structure of the Complex Care system, where everything was closely monitored and evaluated, there has been a significant breakthrough in the way my care has been organised and it has started to transform my life. I can finally look ahead with a greater feeling of control and hope. In a nutshell, I now have the independence that I have always craved because I have been allowed to appoint my own staff to do what I want. I needed something like this to happen and, thankfully, an opportunity came along.

Personalised health budgets have been introduced for people like me and I was adopted onto the pilot scheme. The possibility had been discussed for much of 2011, but Dad thought it better to delay because I was on my bed and unable to go to work. I am desperate to make a success of the venture both for my longer-term well-being and in order to help others who might benefit if the pilot is successful.

Because I could see the potential in what was to come, the discussion period was nerve-wracking. Having had so many setbacks I desperately wanted this new initiative to go my way. I had a number of meetings with Mary, the commissioner, and Ann-Marie from the Cheshire Centre for Independent Living based in Barnton, a village on the north-west side of Northwich. I then started to write up a support plan covering what I needed. I worked on Tuesdays, Wednesdays and Thursdays and thought it would make sense to advertise the post of personal assistant to work for me on Mondays and Fridays so that I could do what I wanted with my days off.

I advertised the position on the Job Centre website. The whole thing was rather scary as I'd never done anything like this before. I interviewed with Jess, my friend Sarah and Andy. I was nervous at first but, as other interviews followed, I started to enjoy myself. There was one incident that I'll never forget. One candidate recognised Andy from his stint in *Emmerdale* and approached him straight away without acknowledging the rest of us. She flung her arms around him and kissed him on the cheek and shrieked, 'I recognise you! You're even more handsome in real life than you are on the telly.' Andy did not know where to look and the rest of us were gobsmacked!

> *Jessica: I'm really proud of Hannah. I've been in the interviews with her and she handles them so well. When I think how nervous she was at first! She comes across as so professional and knows exactly what she's talking about. This is all the more impressive because it's not something that comes naturally to her. Dad and I work in commercial businesses where you have to make money. You have to question everything you're doing. Important decisions are made every day and you have to know exactly what questions to ask when interviewing. Hannah has no experience of that.*

Out of the first round, luckily for me, came Pam, who started in August 2011. It was a significant breakthrough after months of planning. Training was needed and the Cheshire Centre organised courses such as manual handling and basic life support. Pam could start straight away, which helped speed up the process. What was so good about the training was that I was present for all sessions and the PAs were trained around my specific needs, hence the word 'personalised' in the title of the service.

> **Pam (personal assistant):** *I'd done care for the last ten years on and off and had experience of personal care with autistic children, but there has been nothing to match Hannah's situation. My main concern at the start was getting an understanding of the medical equipment. I was scared to death at first, but I was given plenty of help and, like anything else, you get used to it. I also had to get used to working with other carers as rotas overlapped. Sometimes you might be sitting for a couple of hours before Hannah wakes up.*
>
> *Things have changed a huge amount in my time here. We often go on a shopping expedition, which can't be bad! Apart from the routines we need to follow at each end of the day, the rest of the time is there for Hannah to do what she wants. She can direct things more, which is a big improvement and it means that every day is different. You learn to understand when she wants time on her own or whether she wants to be out. I'm always telling her to stop worrying!*

Pam has been excellent. She has been flexible, efficient and good company. The first time I ventured out with her was really strange because I had been used to having two carers with me for so long. We went to the Anderton Boat Lift with Bella. I'm sure that my lovely dog did not appreciate the historical significance of where we took her but I did. The Boat Lift is a vertical link between the River Weaver and the Trent and Mersey Canal, on the edge of Northwich, and was built in 1875. It was recently restored and is a really interesting place not too far away. Dad waved me off as I left the driveway and it must have been really strange for him as well. This was a massive milestone because I was finally experiencing the greatest feeling of freedom that I had felt in 12 years. Once I had a taste of it, I wanted more!

After a couple of months I approached Kate, who had initially looked after me a couple of times when she worked for a care agency.

Kate: *Originally I came via the agency to do night shifts. However, the role developed a lot. I did have experience of care work, largely with adults, but it was still a daunting prospect getting involved with Hannah's care. I had never dealt with the sort of equipment provided so that took a bit of getting used to at the start. Hannah has really benefited from the independence that she has been given through the changes in her care system.*

I decided to make one of my other Complex Care days a PA day and, because I like to socialise with my friends at the weekend, thought it would be a good idea to replace Complex Care with my own staff on a Saturday. Then I could go out without having to plan it weeks ahead. For the first time there might be some spontaneity in my life.

Fran: *Hannah is now reclaiming her independence. She can also surround herself with people she likes and trusts implicitly. A lot of people have come through our door over the last 12 years or so since she returned from Alder Hey. People like Jane the German teacher, and Cynthia have become really good friends. Hannah would never have met those people had she not been ill. There have been one or two you'd have rather not met but, on the whole, they are far outweighed by the nice people. That is life though. In any given group there will be some you get on with and others you don't.*

It was not long before my third full-time appointment followed as Emily joined the team. Emily is lovely and could be trained up very quickly. She had just supported a man who had had a tracheotomy. We managed to get a rota going and I was now using PAs four days a week. Another positive was that I was able to go to my choir group on a Tuesday evening without having to rely on Mum taking me. It wasn't just me who was benefiting from the extra freedom. Mum and Dad were liberated from having to be continually at my beck and call when I wanted to go out anywhere.

A fourth appointment saw the arrival of Vikki and here's what she has to say:

Vikki (personal assistant): *I am from Winnington so I am handy for the work. It's a lot different from my previous job which was in a bakery! I've given up my cut-price loaf perk! I asked a lot of questions and found out many of the answers from Hannah and Pam. It's amazing how much you pick up from just standing watching and now my training's done I'm getting more hands-on experience. I've learned how to move Hannah and both Julie and Karen have been in to help me. [Vikki's done it all really fast!] I think there's going to be a lot of laughs on the way!*

My Monday session is when Hannah goes to the hairdresser and the first trip with me was rather eventful. Before we left Hannah told me how easy it was. Apparently, they never had any problems. However, Hannah was in her manual wheelchair that day. On the way, she asked me to pull over. She was sitting up so much that she was in danger of tumbling over when the car slowed down! We arrived late and had to apologise! If she'll let me take her again I'm thinking of having my hair done at the same time because I go there myself.

Vikki's appointment gave me enough to cover nearly a whole week. She is so easy to talk to and on our first dog walk with Bella we got involved in a discussion about fairground rides. I told Vikki that we had been to Florida when I was 14 and that it had been wasted on me because I hated rides. If I'd known then that I was going to get ill in a year or so then I would probably have gone on every single ride! I talked to Vikki about a trip to Blackpool Pleasure Beach with the Mitchells before I was ill. I remember this day so well. All the others were going on the rollercoaster. They were urging me to go on it and, finally, I gave in. I sat next to Helen and kept thinking, 'I hate everyone for making me do this!' When I got off I felt so sick and knew exactly why I hated these rides! Now I think to myself, 'I want to do all that ride stuff, simply because I can't do it!'

Incidentally – and nothing to do with the book but it's hilarious all the same – Mum went on a log flume once and her glasses fell off into the water! For ages we were getting other people's glasses sent to us as they kept finding further pairs! There must be a lot of people who can't see where they are going at the Pleasure Beach! I've gone off the subject again, sorry!

I don't do the payroll for my personal assistants, but I draw up all the timesheets, write contracts and deal with stock management, so there are extra responsibilities that come with the new age. We must be sure about every step of the journey.

Having the personalised care package has been a hundred times better than before.

Towards the end of 2012 I was invited to talk about my experience of a personalised package on BBC's Radio 5 Live! I was asked if I could get to Media City in Manchester by 6 p.m. A researcher put a few questions to me over the phone and I was told that I would be on just after the news and sport at 6:35. Dad took me and before I left I rang round as many people as possible to tell them to listen in. When we arrived, Dad seemed more excited about seeing the *Match of the Day* set! He was in his element as we went through the plush new buildings and took loads of pictures. He had to wait outside the studio during the live interview so he made sure that the equipment I needed to enable me to speak when not ventilated was on really tight. I couldn't afford it to come off mid-interview because I wouldn't have been able to tell them how to get it back on. As the news was read, I sat thinking how weird it was that I was here waiting to go on national radio. I was surprisingly calm. If I'd have known weeks in advance rather than on the day I would have been proper stressed by now!

The interview seemed to pass in a flash and I was pleased with how it went. So was Dad. On the way back he told me how proud he was of me and how he couldn't understand why I let little things stress me out when I do something like that so well. He told me to store it in the memory bank so that when I was down, it would be another wonderful experience to remember.

Everything's gone well with the new system but at the same time it's been exhausting. It's not all been plain sailing, though, and I think a lot of that is to do with the fact that I am now in charge of my own destiny.

Fran: *Hannah has gone from a situation where other people have been in control to taking control herself. You must remember that she hasn't had such authority at any time in her life, which makes* *it all the more difficult to cope with. She has to organise training and interviews and make countless decisions. Hannah finds it difficult to be assertive. I think she takes after me! It is hard for people to appreciate that. Anything not working properly now is Hannah's responsibility.*

I'm going to be having some employer training and I'm sure I will improve, but I have given serious thought to appointing a manager at some point.

The Primary Care Trust controls the money. They want me to use the budget that was spent on Complex Care for employing other people. They make the final decisions.

Having greater control of my staff means that I have to constantly motivate myself to keep the organisation going, but there is no doubt that it has worked for me so far and I am looking forward to the benefits that it can bring in the future. Typically for Hannah the worrier I am scared about getting too excited about it all, in case it all goes pear-shaped at some stage, but that's just me.

Jessica: *I was talking to someone at work the other day about the things that Hannah takes charge of. If I'm stressed and have a lot on I can just pick up a pen and paper and write down a list of things that need doing. Then I can begin to prioritise and tick things off. Hannah doesn't have that option.*

As well as allowing me more freedom to do things like go out with Bella after work, the arrangement also helps me in more mundane ways. An example was when Sue and Dave came down to discuss the book for the first time. I wanted to keep the visit a secret from Mum, but she would have been horrified to think that they had arrived at an untidy house! It was so nice to be able to say to a personal assistant, 'Can you run the hoover round the living room before Sue and Dave come, please?' It sounds such a small thing, I know, but for far too long my carers have not been allowed to do things like that. It wasn't their fault but the system which restricted them. These restrictions also forbade them from feeding Bella, so if Mum and Dad were away we had to make sure that either Jess or Naomi was always available. My personal assistants can now feed Bella so, in yet another way, life has become that little bit simpler.

I cannot over-emphasise how empowering this new independence and control is for me. The wheel has turned full circle and we are back to the way in which care was directed at me in the early days. It has gone so much better than I could have expected, but we have to be careful. There have been teething problems such as organising the payment of salaries and the recruitment process hasn't been an altogether straightforward situation. Complex Care are still involved with overnight care but there will come a point when we eventually part company. I cannot thank them enough for what I have achieved with them, but I have now reached the stage where I am ready to move on.

One person who has been a big friend to me is Anita:

Anita (Complex Care): I worked at the David Lewis Centre, the Cheshire care home at Alderley Edge. I worked with learning difficulties, epilepsy and autism. I had lots of experience before coming to work with Hannah but nothing like what working with Hannah has given me. I had also worked for many years on night shifts and wanted to get more daytime work. Everyone has been so welcoming and it's been a really nice job. It's been an emotional rollercoaster, though. 2011 was particularly hard and I found myself continually repeating, 'It's going to be OK,' but in the end you're not a miracle worker. It was a case of keeping Hannah's spirits up. There's no doubt overall that Hannah is a lot more confident now. She still worries, but I cannot see that changing! It's just in her nature. She has to make sure that everything is right. The move to having personal assistants was a big worry initially but now Hannah has so much more freedom.

Sometimes it has been difficult to fill the overnight slots and that can be really frustrating, involving endless phone calls. Naomi stepped in once. I'm allowed to use her and Jess in the event of an emergency and pay them for the hours. There have also been occasions when Mum has had to step in.

Anyway, Naomi came home after a night out in Liverpool to hear the news that we had a problem covering the night staff.

Unbeknown to me because I was asleep by then, Mum and Dad gave her the option of taking the hours and the money. I got a shock in the night when I shouted out. Naomi's voice came back, 'What do you want?' and I wondered who it was for a moment. Then I realised! She said, 'Are you gonna die in the next 30 seconds, because I want to put my pyjamas on?'!

Later, there was a beeping from the bottom of the bed which signified that the water bag needed changing. Naomi wondered where the replacements were and I said, 'Under the chair.'

Suddenly I heard this cry: 'Oh no!' I asked what the problem was and she said that there was water all over the room! She had tried to fix the new bag the wrong way round and caused a spillage. She went to get a towel and mopped it up. The carer came in at eight the following morning, at which point a relieved Naomi escaped and went straight to bed, not to be seen until about two o'clock in the afternoon as she slept off her eventful night!

CHAPTER TWENTY
Opportunities to Spread My Wings
'My friend's in a wheelchair and we are stuck in your lift!'

The new dawn in my caring arrangements meant that 2012 was most definitely a year of opportunity. As the nation was celebrating the Queen's Diamond Jubilee, the Olympics and the Paralympics the 'feel-good' factor was coming my way as well!

In January I finally went out for the first time 'on my own', without family or carers chaperoning me, and out of the locality as well. It was over 12 years since I had been admitted to Alder Hey Hospital and, at last, I was off on a big night out! I made the most of it; I was out until three o'clock in the morning! Pam was the first person to take me out and she went for a meal with her husband as my work friends and I celebrated a birthday at a nightclub in the centre of Chester, about 16 miles west of home.

We were able to take my friends there and my sister Naomi was also with us. Pam drove us. No more red tape!

I have to say, Mum and Dad were really good about it. Dad was asking all the usual questions before we went out – 'Have you got this, that and the other?' – but, to their credit, they didn't ring once while we were out or come down when we got back home at around three o'clock in the morning. They proved me wrong because I thought that they would be waiting up for me! The next morning, Mum said they had in fact been awake and she had told Dad to go down and check. He resisted, though, and I think that's really cool.

Howie: *That was the point of having the personal assistants. We could be off duty.*

I had always wanted to go out on my own without my mum and dad. Now it had happened! What a brilliant night, a huge step along my own personal journey back to being as nearly normal as it was possible to be.

The night out reminded me of a previous visit to the same club, with Lizzy, Sarah and Anna. That was an eventful evening! At that stage, I could only go if Mum and Dad took me and we left them not far away from the club as we headed off to celebrate Lizzy's birthday. It must have been about 11.30 when we arrived and we decided to head straight for the top floor. We took the lift up and we were all giggling and laughing as the early alcohol was beginning to take effect. Suddenly there was this awful crashing noise and we stopped! It was a real 'OMG' moment as we got stuck on the top level! One of my friends pressed the emergency button, but there was no response. Many would have panicked but, under the influence of a drink or two already, we thought it was hilarious! However, as soon as the initial frivolity had worn off, we wondered what we could do. Sarah remembered that she had the number for the club reception on her phone. Fortunately, there was a signal. She told a voice at the other end, 'Hi, my friend's in a wheelchair and we're all stuck in your lift!'

We were managing to keep our cool and, in fact, were even filming the experience on our mobiles! The manager came up and couldn't get the doors to part. He tried to wedge them open but without luck. Sarah then rang Dad and told him the news that we were stuck in the lift on the top floor. Mum and Dad headed the short distance to the club and I could just imagine Dad mumbling under his breath! Staff came up to them and started offering them drinks. Instead of worrying about my welfare and the safety of our group they made themselves comfortable on some settees on the top floor and began to have a nice time 'on the house'!

Eventually, we rejoined the outside world, but that wasn't the end of the predicament. There I was on the top floor of the club alongside a lift that had broken down. How was I to get back down? To make matters worse, the club did not have an evacuation chair to carry old or disabled persons down in cases of emergency. They said they would have to ring the fire brigade! Oh my God! My embarrassment at having my parents called into the club was soon replaced by Dad's own as he assessed the situation from behind his drink and realised that the fire brigade might be on the way!

The club then told us that they couldn't get the emergency services without paying for the call-out and, in the end, decided that the only way of solving the problem was to carry me and my chair separately down the stairs! Electric wheelchairs weigh a ton and so the bouncers were called in! As I was moved slowly downstairs, I just remember seeing hundreds of revellers as far as the eye could see and every one of them seemed to be staring in my direction. How I avoided dying of embarrassment that night I just don't know, and it's an occasion that my friends all brought up when we were researching for the book. They've obviously not forgotten it!

Sarah: Yes, it was an interesting night but all's well that ends well because I think we got in free the next time!

In the early months, and even years, of my illness I wouldn't have even dared go out of the house, so visiting places like that nightclub was massive progress. I'd been used to hearing about all the fun that my friends were having and wanted my share of it. I love the atmosphere in clubs and really look forward to my visits. I'm getting much more confident every time I go. I wouldn't have dreamt of behaving like that at one stage. People's reactions are really interesting. Some will say, 'Good on you, love,' or 'What happened to you?' My friends have got pretty good at making answers up.

Lizzy: People try to say 'hello' to her and probably think they are being quite friendly, wanting to kiss her on the cheeks for example.

Kate: They usually leave us alone, but I remember a guy coming over once and offering Hannah a drink. 'Sorry to see you like that, love,' he said, which she found upsetting. It holds her back when people feel sorry for her.

Lizzy: *We were very protective of Hannah at first, but she has got used to all the attention and kind of deals with it in her own way. When she's drunk she sometimes turns sleepy but on other occasions laughs it off and gets on with the fun. On the dance floor you certainly have to watch your toes when she's spinning her chair round and round! If you get in the way it's your own fault!*

Kate: *Hannah can be a liability in her wheelchair if she's had a drink or two! Hold a drink up for her and if you turn round it's gone when you turn back!*

Sarah: *It's hard enough to drive the wheelchair when you are sober, I would think but must be impossible when you've had some. We all find it difficult under the influence of a cocktail or two! Hannah can be very funny when she's out. She'll twizzle round on the dance floor, flashing her lights which is a hoot!*

Kate: *Hannah just loves going out now whereas previously she thought people were judging her. She didn't feel comfortable at first but now she just doesn't care! We've been out a lot over the last few years, in fancy dress at times, and always have a laugh. Once we were all dressed as Christmas trees!*

One of Sarah's claims to fame is that she has got stuck in not one but three lifts with me! The worst of the three was probably the experience in another nightclub. On this occasion it was just Sarah, Lizzy and me out together. I can't remember the exact reason for being out that night, but we may have been celebrating birthdays as Sarah and I were born 11 days apart in March.

This lift was only going to take us up a short distance and Lizzy had walked up the few steps to meet us. It was quite a small lift and had no light in it. When it broke down, Sarah looked through a tiny window and could just see the club's door staff nearby. She tried to attract their attention by banging on the glass and waving. Lizzy came down the stairs to see where we were and Operation Rescue 2 was set in motion. The person who we alerted then had to find someone else to look for the keys. I suppose the length of time spent trapped wasn't long but not being able to see out of the window and being in darkness made it an uncomfortable experience. Sarah couldn't use her phone to ring out on this occasion so it was a bit scary for a moment or two.

The 'hat trick' was achieved at a college in Northwich when we went for a choir practice. This time it featured one of those platform-type lifts which are half open. It kept having mechanical problems, but you could see the trapped people easily. The site manager was regularly being sent for to aid the unfortunate trapped victims!

Lizzy: I think Hannah and Sarah should definitely be banned from being in a lift together!

There was another famous occasion when Mum and Dad were called to help me out. I'll leave it to Naomi to set the scene.

Naomi: Hannah had been out in Liverpool and had got really, really drunk.

She's exaggerating!

Naomi: No, I'm not, and stop interrupting! Hannah was so drunk that she couldn't drive her chair down the road! I was slapping her on the face to try and keep her awake so she could drive her chair.

Howie: It must have been about half past two in the morning. We had gone out for something to eat and were waiting and waiting for the call to take Hannah home when one of her friends called. 'Where are you?' she asked. We told her where we were and asked if there was a problem. 'Erm, can you come across to us. Hannah's having a bit of trouble with her wheelchair.' I asked where they were and headed to Concert Square. I found Hannah fast asleep and making strange noises! There were cobbles on the streets and I had to guide Hannah and her heavy chair over a quarter of a mile by activating the headrest. The streets were lined with drunken Scousers! I kept asking to get past and was apologising over and over again. Eventually we reached the van. Hannah had come round a bit by now. She was able to drive into it, one eye open but hadn't realised that the side door was also open and she nearly drove straight out again!

Not my greatest night! Apparently, I avoided being sick on the journey home, but I paid for it the next day! I was really not well. I have to admit to being drunk in charge of a wheelchair several times! However, I don't see why I can't have a good time like everyone else. One club had a pitcher full of a cocktail. It would normally be enough to pour half a dozen glasses. My friends tell me that I took a straw and drank it all in one go!

I had also started going out to the local pubs with my friends. Not far, but it was good. The Coachman was one destination, just half a mile or so down the road near Hartford railway station. When I first went I said to my friends, 'Now look, I don't want you to be worried about talking honestly about things like boyfriends.' Everything had got too delicate and it was like treading on eggshells. Anna said, 'OK. I've got a question – how do you go to the toilet?' Then we had this massive conversation about going to the toilet! I really appreciate people asking me direct practical questions like that because these are the biggest life-changing things and it helps me to explain them. Incidentally, for an answer to Anna's question, you will have to read on a few more pages!

Susan: *Hannah had to sit back and watch as we learned to drive and started going out with boyfriends... it's absolutely amazing how well she has coped. I often think about that and that many of us would not have stood a chance of coming through the ordeal. I talk a lot about her, how amazing she is to come through, get a degree and a job. When you think what happened and when it happened in her life you assume that many others would not have managed at all. I'll always make an effort to see Hannah for a catch-up or a walk with the dogs. The PA thing is so good and I'm really pleased that she has finally been able to organise something. Every little step she makes is important and we are thrilled when she makes them.*

Rosanne: *Yes, it was often difficult when you were doing things that she was never going to be able to manage. Hannah didn't want us to hide anything from her, which made it even harder.*

Kate: *We didn't want to upset her, but if we hadn't talked about these things we'd have had nothing to talk about!*

Anna: *I tell Hannah everything so she never gets left out. I know that it's sometimes hard for her to bear but I think it's for the best.*

I definitely don't want people to hide things from me just to spare my feelings because I genuinely want to know how they are doing. If a friend gets a new boyfriend I'm glad for her but deep down I hate the situation. It's a massive obstacle for me. I get peculiar feelings in the pit of my stomach. It's not jealousy, more a sadness and hurt that I've not had that same experience. I don't want to spoil my friends' excitement by telling them how I feel at times like this, but I am able to talk more honestly from time to time with a friend or a carer. I'll try to describe my true feelings to them and it can be reassuring.

Taking me out was a big novelty for my friends at first and, as ever, they were great about it and couldn't wait for the next time. In those days you could smoke indoors and I remember that on one occasion there were some people smoking near where we were. I got a bit stressed and had to leave the pub. Outside, I immediately burst into tears.

Rosanne: *We thought it was great to get Hannah out of the house and down to the pub. That was the first time that she had been able to go there with her friends.*

I don't have any qualms now in social situations; I love talking to people, but it has taken 13 years and I can't thank my friends enough for encouraging me. What I have been through has undoubtedly been life-changing for me, but I never forget that it has been life-changing for my friends as well, particularly those from school days who knew me as an able-bodied person. Credit to them, they have always wanted to treat me as normal and keep things normal and that has meant so much to me.

Before I move on I should come clean about how frustrated my friends get when we are ordering something. I take forever to decide!

Lizzy: *Hannah can take an age to decide the simplest of things such as what drink or pizza to have. We just ignore her now and let her decide for herself. It's much easier that way!*

Kate: *Hannah and I went out for a meal the other day. It took her half an hour to decide what she wanted! She can be so indecisive, just like she was when we first got to know her.*

Anna: *She can also take ages choosing on a Friday night when we order a takeaway from her house.*

None of us are perfect!

CHAPTER TWENTY-ONE
Here, There and Everywhere

'They hid some wine under my coat and let me take it in!'

As well as getting to enjoy pub and nightclub life I also managed to get to various concerts. I've always loved music, and not just Robbie Williams! I went with some friends from work to see the Wanted, the English–Irish boy band, at the Echo Arena in Liverpool. Pam accompanied me on this occasion and my drunken mates were very naughty. They hid some wine under my coat and let me take it in. I'm obviously useful for some things!

There was also a trip to the Echo to see the American group, the Backstreet Boys. Naomi didn't want to go so I went with one of my PAs. To be honest, I think the Backstreet Boys were a bit after her time, but she was really excited when I invited her and loved the evening. It was another big step for me and, once again, showed the value of having personal assistants who could respond to my wishes. It meant that I could do things when I wanted to and it didn't matter if no one else wanted to join me. When I got home after the show, those who had been a bit 'iffy' about the event were suddenly jealous when I told them how brilliant it was and they kept saying, 'Oh, take me next time!'

I also went to see the lovely Will Young in concert in Delamere Forest. He was really good and, despite all the rain we had had, I didn't get my wheelchair stuck in the mud! There's no way I'm going to let my situation hold me back and everywhere is pretty much disabled-friendly these days.

A less memorable trip to the Etihad Stadium, scene of so many exciting Manchester City games, was the night all the Roses went to see Bruce Springsteen, the American singer-songwriter also known as 'The Boss'. Before I alienate all those Springsteen fans out there, it wasn't the concert itself that was the problem but the trials and tribulations we had getting there! Despite Dad trying every trick in the book, we couldn't get a disabled parking spot at the stadium so we had this brilliant idea of parking at Jess's place and walking the rest of the way. It was a ten or fifteen-minute walk. Great idea at the time! Typically of the lousy summer weather it was throwing it down with rain. Dad was upset big-time because Naomi couldn't get out of work until five o'clock. We were then stuck in serious traffic jams in the city centre and Bruce was on at seven! Naomi kept reassuring us: 'He won't come on that early!' Dad, meanwhile, was getting really bad road rage and shouting at people. He was up close and personal with the cars in front. You could have cut the tension with a knife. Mum was having a go at Dad who then had a go back while Naomi shouted at Dad for shouting at Mum! We were like the family from hell! It goes to show that, however much our lives have been upturned by my illness, we are still a typically moaning and whingeing family and that is rather reassuring.

Once we finally got to the car parking area near Jess's there was a further debate sparked by Mum saying she'd drop us off at the stadium and come back to park. We decided to stick to the original plan and walk the rest of the way. It was still raining, Dad had a bad leg to make his mood even worse and I was, of course, in my wheelchair!

I found progress difficult because the road was really bumpy and the cars were coming very close. I was trying to drive the electric wheelchair and Dad was getting even more impatient as his leg gave him more and more grief. We arrived at the stadium like drowned rats. Dad directed us to where we were supposed to be and we split up as I had to go into a particular area with Mum. I was zooming around and calling to people, 'Excuse me!' I wouldn't have asserted my authority in this way in the early years. It's all part of the confidence thing, I suppose. We missed the first song but it didn't matter that much as he's not my favourite act. He was really good though and on stage for about four hours.

The problems did not end there as getting back out was an absolute nightmare. There were more 'excuse me's' along the way. People react quite differently. Sometimes they get really irritated if you catch their foot or something, but others help me by shouting, 'Let this lady through, come on now,' and things like that. The journey back to the car was much quicker as I had got used to the path. However, there was a car parked over one of the 'drop kerbs' and Jess was banging on the bonnet, shouting, 'Excuse me, my sister is trying to get through. She can't use her legs, you know.'

That sort of reaction makes me realise how proud I am of my family for sticking up for me. There was another time when we were at Wetherspoon's. I came out and a man who followed me said, 'God, love. You didn't need to get that legless.' Jess replied, 'Excuse me, that would be really funny if she wasn't paralysed and on a ventilator.' Despite our moaning we are a really good team who overcome problems together just like many families do in normal circumstances.

Trips out were becoming much more commonplace as my confidence improved and continued to benefit from personalised health care. I celebrated Grandpa's 90th birthday by travelling over to Manchester with my personal assistant. We took him to Roma's, the Italian café which was about five minutes away from his house, and where he used to go with Grandma. He decided to have the Super Toastie because that's what he always had with Grandma. They used to go there so much that someone paid for them once. He's not been back for ages. I tried to treat him but he refused to let me and bought lunch. Then we had an ice cream before we brought him home and he went out for tea with Mum and Dad.

I love the freedom that my outings can give and there was a particularly pleasurable example on the 13th anniversary of my going into hospital, 20 May 2012. I went up to Sue and Dave's neck of the woods, to the Pleasure Beach in Blackpool. In case you haven't been, it's a massive amusement park opposite the South Pier and just the place for a fun-loving girl like me!

I was up there with Dad and Naomi and the reason we went was because it was Vicki from work's birthday. They went on the Saturday as they were going on a night out in Blackpool. I was feeling a bit low because I couldn't do what they were doing so it meant a lot to me when they invited me to come and join them on the Sunday. It was such a nice day. We went to Madame Tussauds and on the arcades and it was so lovely to think that Vicki had included me in the plans. I was upbeat because I realised that I had a lovely new group of friends who liked to do nice things with me.

Tia: Hannah and I have been out socially with friends from work, including our joint birthday celebrations in Chester. We are in a close-knit group who plan lovely nights out. Hannah gets the drinks in, laughs and jokes just like the rest of us.

It was particularly good to be in Blackpool on that day because last year's anniversary had been so rubbish on my bed. Eventually, my workmates went home suffering from a hangover and we looked for fish and chips! We couldn't find a shop which didn't have a step so Dad bought some and we ate them in the car. Then we drove round a corner and immediately found a shop minus a step!

Jess loves my friends at work and they always try to include me in their plans. In fact, I'm gutted when I have to miss an evening out because I cannot bear to miss out on the gossip! Something was arranged while we were on holiday and I couldn't go. I was really upset but they said, 'You've got to have holidays, Hannah! There'll be other times!' Every day when I get home from work I think how lucky I am.

Fran: They accept Hannah as she is because that's what she was like when she met them.

There was yet another breakthrough in June when I went out with my friends without Mum, Dad, my sisters or any carers. For a long time my friends had been talking about taking me out for the day. Suddenly, they said, 'What do you want to do next Sunday?' They suggested going to Leeds. Mum and Dad were at a cousin's birthday party in Rochdale that day and Mum, in particular, put her foot down at the thought of us crossing the Pennines into Yorkshire. That was a bit too ambitious for her liking!

In the end we settled on Chester. The trip was made possible by the fact that my specially adapted car can now be driven by anyone (with a driving licence!). Sarah had offered to do the honours and she came along with Anna and Jim, Anna's boyfriend. I got myself ready and we loaded up. Sarah got into the driver's seat and discovered, to her horror, that she could not move the car. She had not driven an automatic very much before.

Sarah: *This is going to come back to haunt me, I can see! In my defence I'd had little experience of an automatic and I'd never driven that particular vehicle!*

The four of us were all set to go but stood stationary on my drive. Mum and Dad were in Rochdale and I had sent my personal assistants and carers home!

After some thought, Anna rang Dad to ask how to start the car. I had been thinking how worried Dad was in the first place. For him to now find out that this had happened was heaping more anguish on him, but in the end, we had no choice. He talked Anna through the process over the phone. Suddenly, the car moved! I cannot remember Anna's exact words to Dad but they were along the lines of 'Hooray, we're moving... see you later!'

We went to a pub for lunch, after which we called on two friends of ours who had recently had a baby. Unfortunately, my catheter bag had to be emptied but my friends stepped in. The next problem was getting up the two big steps that led into the house. Mum and Dad would have worried had they been there, but my intrepid friends did a run at the house and got me in! Our friends had nice cream carpets. It was a wet day and the others wiped their feet on the mat. We had to put a towel down for me and I drove backwards and forwards over it to clean and dry my wheels! It made me laugh and Sarah thought it was hilarious.

I had a lovely day and it was another massive milestone on my journey. Mum rang twice, once when we were in the pub and again at our friends' house. Mum and Dad were at home when we got back. The trip made me realise how much I was freeing myself of the shackles that had burdened me for years. Granted, my physical state had not changed, but thanks to technology, changes in my care system and the sheer wonderful bloody-mindedness of my friends, I had been able to do something normal that I would have done as an able-bodied person.

Spurred on by this successful mission, Sarah and I went out the very next day! She took me to Delamere Forest, about half way to Chester, and we were able to walk our dogs. Sarah's mum came along as well. Sarah drove the van again, this time without any problems. (Promise I won't mention that again, Sarah!)

> **Celia:** *Hannah loves going out with Bella. I tend to see her at her house or go to a café or we will take our dogs out because I have dogs as well. During one particularly bad period Hannah said to me, 'I can't wait to get back out with Bella.' I remember thinking that an exercise we take for granted every day is a big deal for Hannah.*

Things were going so well that Mum and Dad felt able to spend a weekend away together in Stratford-upon-Avon. I had the most amazing time without them! On the Saturday, Emily took Naomi and me to Cheshire Oaks for some retail therapy. We also went to Pizza Hut and the cinema before returning home to watch the Muppets on DVD! More was to follow the next day as Naomi and I went with Vikki to the Trafford Centre.

> **Lizzy:** *Having the sort of PAs she's got makes it much easier for a shopping expedition or a night out. She has people around her who are similar in age and attitude and want to enjoy the same things as Hannah.*

These experiences have all been so good that I now feel as confident as I can ever remember. In fact, I'm worried that the bubble is going to burst! What a big step forward...

Jessica: One Saturday, I saw Mum at my grandma's. She told me that Dad was at home on his own. It sounds no big deal in most families, but I thought that was unbelievable; I'd thought it was something we would never see in our family life again. Things are happening, though. Mum can go to see Grandma; Hannah can take Bella for a walk. If you'd told me five years ago that all this activity was going to happen I genuinely wouldn't have believed you. It seemed difficult to see any way out of our situation at that stage. There was no hope and it was an unsustainable situation.

This is all wonderful news to be able to share with you, but there was another episode recently which brought home the stark reality that surrounds me day in, day out. No one was to blame but what happened really upset me. It all came about from my habit of listening in on other people's conversations. This time I became a victim of my own curiosity!

I was in the living room at the end of a lovely day. I'd been out shopping which was really nice and it put me in a really good mood. Then I heard Jess talking in the kitchen about Greece. I shouted through, 'Who's going to Greece?' The answer came back, 'Me and Naomi.'

That short answer made me feel really sad, and then anger set in. I don't know why. I wanted my sisters to do things, but I felt so frustrated that I couldn't join them. I decided that I didn't want to speak to anyone so I just shut the door and sat on my own. England were playing Sweden in the Euro 2012 football championships that evening and Mum, Dad and I were going to watch the match on television. Suddenly I lost my appetite for football. Within minutes I had got myself in such a state.

Naomi had rung me around lunchtime from work asking if the two of us could go to the Trafford Centre. She was really keen to go and kept pleading with me. It was unusual for her to ring at that time of day so I thought it was a bit strange. I told her that I was going to watch the football and was a bit tired. She kept asking me to change my mind.

I later found out that Naomi had told Mum in the car on the way home from work that she and Jess were going away for a few days. It all clicked into place. Naomi knew I was going to find out about Greece that night and it was her way of wanting to make things right with me. She felt bad about going away without me but wanted to be there for Jess as well.

I hated myself for being like that because I don't ever want to appear bitchy and resentful and make others feel bad for what they are doing. I would hate them to feel that way. I could fully understand why they wanted to go on holiday. Nevertheless, I did feel horrible. If this illness had not overtaken me we would have been planning those few days in Greece as a threesome.

That evening Jess and Naomi decided they wanted to go to Cheshire Oaks, a designer outlet shopping centre just off the M53 near Ellesmere Port. They asked me to come with them. Normally I'd have bitten their hands off, but on this occasion, I just wasn't in the mood. Jess asked if I was mad with them. Anyway, they went and I sat at home under my duvet feeling upset. Mum came in and said she had got something lovely for tea. She saw that I was heartbroken.

I'm always going to have those times when it hurts not to be able to do things. As the eldest child in the family I would have ordinarily experienced everything first, but in so many ways I'm missing out and that's hard to take. Mum pulled up a chair, but I told her I wanted to be by myself. She insisted we watch the football together. I said no, and then I got really upset. I know I can go to Greece in the future because I've had holidays abroad, but everything now is such an effort and it just wouldn't fit in well for Jess and Naomi on this occasion. It's just the way it is. I can't just hop on a plane and everything has to be organised for me like a military operation. In my mind I went beyond Greece and started to miss things that I couldn't do any more like putting make-up on or slipping my pyjamas on to come down and watch television. I got sucked back into the self-pity thing. It's particularly hard if you've been able to do those things in your life because you know what it's like. I always used to sleep with my hands under the pillow, for instance. I clearly remember how I used to do things for myself, how things felt... No longer.

At times like this, and thankfully they don't occur too often, I have to keep telling myself that there's so much I *can* do. It must be hard for Mum because I know how much it hurts me when she is upset. We are so similar. In the end we both finished up crying! Most times I'm really upbeat but then a reality check like this comes from nowhere and hits me hard. I get so deflated and a horrid feeling comes into my stomach. You just don't know what to do about it. When I'm like this I'll often get on the phone to Anna, who is always so practical. When you need someone to just agree with you she does it fine! When I rang her about Greece she was in Tesco. She rang back later but the moment had gone. However, it was still good to listen to her.

Initially, I didn't tell anyone else about the Greece thing because I didn't want to come across as a moaner or a spoiled brat. However, a few days later I was just getting up and told Alison and Anita, who were on duty. Alison replied, 'Do you know what, Hannah, you'll be going to Greece by yourself one day anyway!' Anita backed her up. Alison continued, 'Since I've been looking after you I've seen you do a million things.' It's typical of her to be so positive. 'I've been here from the beginning and I'll be here when you're 50!' she told me once. Alison's so organised as well. She always gets me going so quickly in the morning and has me ready for bed quickly at night.

Mum and Dad don't go away often overnight but I'm really relieved if I have Alison here when they do. She just knows me so well. She is almost like family and I can be totally myself with her. She has a great knack for putting everything into perspective.

Another type of support comes from Chris Hynes. Chris, Liz and their family have always been lovely friends of ours and it was Chris who asked me if he could try out something called reiki on me. Reiki is a system of natural healing developed in the 1920s by a Japanese Buddhist, Mikao Usui. The method of receiving treatment from a practitioner like Chris is very simple. The recipient has to be as comfortable as possible and the practitioner gently places their hands non-intrusively in a sequence of positions which cover the whole body. Chris will spend 45 minutes to an hour with me each week and has been doing it for about six years now. Energy is channelled and it has a really calming influence on me. Dad received it for a while as well and, more recently, Chris gave him some extra exercises to help cope with his dodgy knee.

I really look forward to the sessions because I can chill out and have some 'me time'. Chris is good to talk to and I can tell him about my week. He's also very good at giving advice. If I'm down I'll talk to him and he often comes up with some help.

> **Chris Hynes:** *It's a bit like acupuncture but without the needles. Hannah has come on a million miles and deserves everything that she has achieved. It's so gratifying to see and a privilege to work with her. For all Hannah says I have done things to help her she has done at least as much if not more for me and I thank her for her part in my journey.*

Typical of the generosity of Chris and his family, they invited Jess, Naomi and me to their house for an evening of music. Their son, Oliver, really likes this band called the Candle Thieves who come from Peterborough. If you pay they'll come and do a concert in your kitchen! The Hynes's kitchen is a perfect venue. Even better, and I don't want to appear rude, they just invited the three of us – Mum and Dad stayed behind at home! It was so nice that the three of us were out together. It was a really good evening, hot, and we had the patio doors open. The Candle Thieves were fabulous. Liz did Mexican food and Oliver invited about 20 of his friends. Chris even recorded the 'concert' and put it on YouTube.

Chris's reiki sessions help me cope with things like Jess and Naomi's Greek holiday. You can sit and cry as much as you want, but in the end there's nothing you can do except try to be positive. Next time they go it might not feel so bad. I must never forget that now I've got my PAs and friends who want to take me away. I'm going to have more opportunities of my own.

CHAPTER TWENTY-TWO

More Hospital

'It just topped off an already frustrating day.'

Always at the back of my mind throughout 2012 was the issue of my kidney stone. Despite all the good things that were happening in my life, my instinctive need to worry was never far from the surface.

I had gone back for the first of the follow-up operations early in 2012 and felt much better about the experience this time. It was nice to see familiar faces among the nursing staff, including Jenny who was in on everything in November and with whom I have shared many girly chats! I was determined that I wouldn't go back into the same bed as before.

As with life in general, the progress of the kidney stone's destruction was proving far from straightforward. After the second blasting I was told that the stone had got smaller. On the Friday before the Backstreet Boys concert in April I rang Southport Spinal Injuries to get an update because I'd not heard about my next visit, for my third blasting session. It was a good job that I did because they told me that I had been booked in for the following Wednesday. This made me a bit cross and annoyed because I hadn't heard about it and wouldn't have known had I not rung up. At least I was going to get it sorted. I rang work and they were, as ever, very understanding.

The doctor then announced that I had to go in for an X-ray on the Tuesday to check on the progress of getting rid of the stone. They booked me in for half past eleven despite the fact that the unit shut between noon and two o'clock and appointments always ran late. I was cross because I knew that I wasn't likely to get in before the midday break and already had another appointment in the afternoon. They must have gauged my mood because they rang another department in the hospital and got me an earlier X-ray appointment there.

The hospital asked me if I wanted to see the X-ray. 'Don't be optimistic about it, it hasn't worked,' they said. It was not what I wanted to hear, particularly after the better news received last time. The doctor explained that sometimes you cannot really tell until the fourth blasting. It was not a good way of going about things for someone like me who needs plenty of reassurance. I went away feeling downhearted. There was clearly plenty of mileage left in this saga and it was eating into me mentally.

Next stop was the Walton Centre in Liverpool. I had got referred there about seven or eight years ago when I had started to get blurred vision in one eye. I just woke up with it one day and we couldn't work out what was causing it. Dad was worried enough to get me to the eye hospital at Leighton. When I went for my appointment the optic nerve was swollen so they recommended that I see a neurologist. This was easier said than done and we couldn't sort out an appointment for ages. Dad was getting increasingly concerned so we went through BUPA in the end. They referred me to the Walton Centre.

It was suggested that I had something called neuromyelitis optica, also known as Devic's disease. This is an autoimmune condition where your immune system attacks your spinal cord. Those diagnosed with it will have had an episode in both their spine and their eye. Obviously I had the attack on my spine all those years ago. Now it was my eye's turn to cause concern.

The Walton Centre examined me, but the antibodies that would have indicated Devic's disease weren't there. Luckily my vision went back to normal but not before the experts declared that this was a very rare disorder. They put me on a research study and over the years more people have come forward to say that they've had something similar. Every case has been slightly different and some have experienced the eye problem before the spine. Compared to others within the research study mine had been a severe case. I was put on medication designed to lower my immune system. It's not proven, but it's very likely that it stops further attacks. If I could cross my fingers I would, but thankfully, I've not had an episode since those days. They are not 100% sure that it is Devic's, but they are treating it as if it is. I am now watched by both the spinal and neurological branches of medicine and have to be careful to report any further changes in my eyes. This is all moving on from transverse myelitis, the initial condition, which is basically an attack on your spine.

There is a Devic's support group in the hospital and we have all been told that the experts have over-diagnosed the condition in many cases. This showed that a lot of suspected cases weren't Devic's but were more associated with other conditions like MS.

Howie: *The Walton Centre did loads of tests, but the profile of antibodies found in the blood wasn't wholly consistent with a diagnosis of Devic's. It's probably as close as it gets to a definitive answer. Hannah is certainly being treated for that. The term 'transverse myelitis' describes a symptom rather than a cause.*

I had a lot of appointments at Walton on that particular day. During my visit I saw a specialist nurse, a doctor, a counsellor and a physiotherapist among others. The whole situation was, inevitably, very tiring. There was a guy there who was a charity worker and we talked for a while. He asked me when I was last at Walton. I said about six months ago. His reply stunned me: 'Well, you obviously didn't see the dietician, did you?'

That was such a horrible thing to say. One of the things that I have found the hardest since becoming ill has been being unable to do voluntary exercise. Before it all happened I had been the one of the three sisters in the Rose family who did the most sport. Not being able to do it any more often hurts. My friends can go to the gym or play netball. Jess might go for a run at a moment's notice. I know there's nothing I can do about rectifying that situation, but it still makes life really difficult for me. When the guy said what he said it just topped off an already frustrating day for me.

My next chat was with the doctor and everything was fine, then the occupational therapist. They were impressed that I'd now got a team of personal assistants. I felt really good about that and my spirits lifted again. They asked me questions about what difference it had made to my life and were genuinely excited for me. The occupational therapist said she worked at the University of Liverpool and asked me if I fancied doing some public speaking and talking to large groups. She wanted me to speak to the students about empowering their lives, as she felt that my experiences could inspire them. It was a really positive suggestion which I was more than happy to accept and I hope that it will happen.

That proved a positive end to a day which seemed to have gone on for ever and I was shattered by the time I got home. Dad was away for a couple of nights so I am ashamed to admit that I took my feelings out on Mum. I had been out from about ten o'clock in the morning until six in the evening and poured all the bad, frustrating side of a long and arduous day out to her. It was obviously my way of getting it all off my chest and Mum didn't deserve to be the target, but it wasn't the first time by any means that we had both been in that situation. When we went to bed I shouted at Mum because she had told Dad on the phone that the blasting wasn't working and I always like to tell him how things are going. It was a bit of an immature response from me really. We said 'goodnight' to each other, but I realised how horrible I'd been. We had a long chat until about one o'clock and, not for the first time, both of us were crying. Mum and I are very similar and we easily get upset for each other. I must have been really crabby and horrible because I didn't even mention what the lady from the university said about speaking to their students. That was not fair to Mum, but when I finally told her the next day she was thrilled for me.

At work next morning I was really tired. The effect of the previous day had caught up on me. I told Tia how difficult it had been. She suggested that we go out for a chat so we went into the rest area near our office. I got upset, which is a rarity for me at work because I just want to appear normal. It was undoubtedly a build-up of things over the last 24 hours. I was definitely over-tired.

The rest area at work is many things but not very private. The next thing I knew was that this lovely senior member of staff came out and offered me the use of his office, saying that he wasn't going to need it again for a couple of hours. He said that

Tia and I were free to use it as it would be more private. How lovely was that? Tia was brilliant with me and cheered me up.

> **Tia:** *There are times at work when I can see that Hannah is not focused and I will ask her what she's thinking. 'Nothing,' she will often reply but I will persevere. 'Come on, what's wrong?' Normally she wants to concentrate on her work, but there are times when an issue away from the workplace will get her down. She gets easily deflated and angry. I will say, 'Hannah, I'm your friend. I'm here to listen and I'll give you my advice.' She will break down on occasion and I'll say, 'Come on, let's go and find somewhere quiet.' Then it's time for me to cheer her up. Perhaps I'll make up a little song or make her laugh. She'll respond and let me give her my advice.*

The kidney stone preyed on my mind when I wasn't busy, but as spring moved into summer, I knew that there was a family holiday to look forward to. I love planning well in advance and having all that time to get excited. The five of us had booked to travel to Normandy by ferry for a week in August.

I went for another check-up at Southport about two weeks before we were due to set off on holiday. On the way to Southport I asked Mum if we could go to Primark and the shops in Southport after the appointment. She said we didn't have time, which put me in a bad mood. I had the stress of the consultation to deal with so I wasn't feeling good at all. It was also Vikki's first difficult trip as a personal assistant. She hadn't seen me upset before so it was hard for her.

I didn't want to know anything about the progress or otherwise of the kidney stone because I just wanted to go on holiday. It was not a good moment, therefore, when the doctor said that they needed to get me into hospital quickly. The blasts had not worked and surgery was needed. Mum told him that we were going on holiday. He started going on about the insurance and us being able to get our money back for a cancellation! It was really not what I wanted to hear!

Mum insisted that we needed the holiday. We had not been on one for two years. The doctor told us that I would need a big operation and would be in for a while. My heart sank. I just could not take it in. This stone issue just did not want to go away. All the negative attention took the pleasure out of looking forward to the holiday.

As we came away, Mum decided that, after all, we should go to the shops! On arriving home we brought Dad up to date before ringing Stephen Bentley. Stephen was, as ever, very sympathetic and said he would come into the hospital with me on the next occasion, after our holiday. He said he would make sure we asked every question we needed to and get things sorted out. In January 2013 I had a five-hour operation at the Whiston Hospital on Merseyside. They did not use keyhole surgery and removed about 75% of the stone. The remainder was taken out a few weeks later in a second operation. The hospital doctors and nurses were brilliant.

I had got myself into such a state though. This is one thing I'm not proud of. I have to sort myself out at times like this and maybe even consider some kind of counselling. I just wanted to go away without having to consider hospital too much, but the doctor had completely freaked me out. I couldn't concentrate on my work. My head felt as if it was about to explode. Tia, as ever, was brilliant. Her view was, 'Just try and forget about it because you're going on a nice holiday.'

A couple of days later I had a really good laugh with my friends at work. When I got back home I had a bit of a meltdown. I needed to get back on to my bed to be changed. Despite the memories of my fun day at work still being clear in my mind I must have been on the edge emotionally because something pushed me over it. There had been the stress of the hospital visit, problems I had been experiencing recruiting more carers and I also had to have my catheter changed.

As I lay on my bed being changed I found, not for the first time, that something I could not do, namely change myself, had suddenly triggered strong emotions from nowhere. It was not the best preparation for a family holiday, but I'll tell you how that went a little later!

CHAPTER TWENTY-THREE
Glass Half-Full

'An angel sent to give us hope.'

My good friend Andy was contacted by the Back-Up Trust, a charity that helps people who have suffered spinal cord injury. He agreed to attend one of their courses. 'It's just the thing you need,' he said. 'You meet a mentor who talks to you and helps you. It brought me back to life.'

This set me thinking. I was interested in doing some mentoring and Back-Up invited me to do some training. It was strange because once I got there I realised that I would benefit from receiving some mentoring as well. Although my family and friends have been so supportive of me through my illness they cannot fully understand what I'm going through because they haven't experienced it first-hand.

Back-Up's mentoring service paired me up with a 31-year-old lady who had a spinal cord injury when she was 16. She didn't have the same level of injury as me; she could move her arms, but it was still good to talk to someone. I was really nervous when I rang her as I wasn't sure what to ask and thought that there might be awkward silences. It didn't take us long to realise that we had loads in common and couldn't stop talking. In fact, we were on the phone for over an hour! She was further advanced than me in terms of her rehabilitation so it was great to be able to ask her if what I was feeling was normal. We had about ten sessions over the phone. I gradually stopped feeling embarrassed and began to look forward to our next chat.

One of the topics we discussed was how, when we confide in our mums, we don't want to upset them and so sometimes don't say how we are really feeling. My mum had never spoken to a family member of another person who had a spinal cord injury and eventually the two met up. They really enjoyed talking to each other. We weren't supposed to meet up but we did and it was brilliant.

I must admit that before I became a mentee I was sceptical about the system's use. I thought that it wouldn't change a thing and, in fact, might make things worse for me. I couldn't have been further from the truth. Now I feel less isolated and much more positive. It has helped me to get things off my chest and I'm really grateful to the lady who I met. She was equally positive:

> **Mentor:** *Hannah was an easy person to mentor because she is so chatty and bubbly. She is also very articulate and knew what she wanted to get out of our sessions. Hannah started a new job during the mentoring process and it was great to see her approach it with a newfound confidence as a result of our chats.*

A mentor is there to listen and not judge, but it's so easy to get emotionally involved. It can be very rewarding, but things don't always fall into place easily. Stephen asked me a few years ago if I would mind visiting a boy, younger than me, in Warrington Hospital. He'd had a trampolining accident where he had landed awkwardly and broken his neck. I went to see him but, to be honest, it was a bit awkward. He had just had his accident. On this particular occasion, I'm not sure he was ready for me to be there talking and supporting him.

There's also a 15-year-old girl. She received her injury when she was two years old, so she doesn't remember life as an able-bodied person. Her mum and dad wanted her to meet someone else in a similar situation, but it wasn't really that straightforward. She was shy and I felt that there was more that could have been gained from our conversation.

Another girl had an accident in which she broke her neck. She is where I used to be and is very, very low. Like me, she does not believe that she will ever get a life again. I remember all too well how bad I felt at the point where she is now. I wasn't in a good place. I know that she won't want to go out and meet anyone. She cannot speak at the moment and I feel so bad for her. She was very upset and didn't want to go on. I've been there, particularly the period in my bed in 2011. I'd never had a year like that in the whole 12 years since I became ill. A girl once asked me, 'How do you tell people how to do your make-up and hair?' Nowadays, I don't even think about it. I just give them instructions as a matter of routine.

As soon as you discover that there is something wrong with you it's natural that you become aware of other people with the same problems. Whether it is dyslexia or hay fever, there is always someone else, and until you are in that situation, you may never come across them. Soon after coming home, I learned that there was a guy nearby who had been a pilot. I was put in contact with him. He had been having a day off on the beach when he was hit by a wave. He's in the same situation as me and only living just down the road!

The Back-Up Trust, incidentally, was responsible for creating one of the more amusing situations that I have ended up in. It certainly rivalled the famous occasion when I tipped over in the flower bed! I must have been around 19 at the time and, through the Trust, went rally driving in Wales. It was so good! I had this off-road car which I could steer using a Possum through my helmet. I was lifted into it and had a man perched on the back. Dad, meanwhile, had to follow on a tiny quad bike.

We drove it round a country park, past people having a normal day out and I was really getting into it. It was so much fun! As my speed increased the car suddenly hit a rock and tipped on its side before landing in a dip. Thankfully, I wasn't injured and couldn't stop laughing as I lay there. We needed a Land Rover to pull us out and it took ages to get back to Mum at the start line. She couldn't believe what had happened.

There is always hope to be found in adversity. Quite recently, there have been a number of developments which have made me realise even more that I can use my experience to help and advise others.

Dr Selby, my lovely and brilliant consultant from intensive care at Alder Hey, came to my 21st birthday party. We are still good friends and he invited me to be part of a steering group at the hospital helping to advise on adjusting from hospital back into the home environment, something that I have plenty of views on! The group was specially formed for a student doing a Ph.D. in Chester. Her research was based on making the transition for people on long-term ventilation. I've been to a couple of meetings and it has been really good.

> **Fran:** *When Hannah turns up to take part in the steering group they are thrilled to see her because she is a success story. Considering how bad she was in intensive care she has probably turned out to be one of their greatest success stories because she is out and about doing things. That's what Dr Selby said when he came to Hannah's 21st birthday.*

The first time I went with Pam. The meeting was held in the transitional care unit at Alder Hey. Since I left the hospital, they have rigged up a bedroom so you can practise going home. I was both nervous and excited and looking forward to seeing Dr Selby again.

When I was being driven to the meeting I got to thinking about my mum making the journey to and from Hartford day after day for months. Then I thought about my dad and how he used to stop in Ronald McDonald House. They wouldn't have had many nights together during that period. What a sacrifice they had made for me. I didn't have a clue about all that at the time. I was cocooned in my own world and it was strange to think how life went on all that time.

As plans so often do with me, our plan ahead of the meeting went awry. We followed my satnav but it didn't work because the transitional care unit is not exactly in Alder Hey so we were driving round for a bit. I was still the first there, though, which doesn't often happen. I was a good 20 minutes before the others. Apart from the student and Dr Selby, there was a consultant from Manchester Hospital and a couple of other people. I felt useful and my contribution was valued. They were impressed by what I had to say and excited that I was now employing my own team of carers. Meetings are to be held every six months so they're not going to happen too often, but it was nice to be part of something that I cared about and also good to be appreciated. Despite it being early days at the moment this will, hopefully, be something that will enable me, in the longer term, to make a positive contribution to help others.

It was the first time that I had seen Dr Selby for about three years. On that occasion we went to Ronald McDonald House because we had raised money for the House at a coffee morning. During my visit to Alder Hey I went back up to have a look at intensive care. I was really nervous as I heard the buzzer which would alert one of the nurses to let me in. I was careful not to get too excitable as I had to remember that it was a sad place containing lots of poorly children. I met some familiar faces, which was really nice, and I gave them all a cheery welcome. I also went to my old room where they were doing a training session for the doctors and Dr Selby went in and interrupted them. He told them that it had been my room for such a long time and asked if I could have a look inside. My main impression was that it looked so much smaller than I remembered. I got a bit emotional about it and felt weird because everything that had happened back then seemed like a dream.

Another step forward was in the form of a chance encounter. I went for a check-up at Southport on a beautiful sunny Monday in March 2012. I had made a number of plans for the rest of the day following the appointment but they were not to be fulfilled. As I eased my way out of the lift, a woman approached me, eager to talk. Her son had been admitted to the spinal unit the day before. I told her that I would come back after my appointment and duly did. I listened as the story unfolded. Seven months ago, the young man had been in an accident in Israel whilst out cycling and received spinal injuries, slightly higher in intensity than mine. He had just been moved to England for further treatment.

The lady wanted to know about anything and everything and I had arrived, from her point of view, at exactly the right time. She asked me a lot of questions about my electric wheelchair and I found myself giving all kinds of advice to her. She took me to her son's bedside where I met him and his wife. He also had a baby son. The experience took me back to when I had been in his position, something that I had largely forgotten about. He asked about lots of things such as what arrangements I had for care and how I managed to speak so well. I felt heartbroken for the family, but it was heartening to see how appreciative they were of my interest and support.

The mother described me as 'an angel sent to give us hope' while her injured son admitted that my presence at his bedside had helped him. All my remaining plans for the day went out of the window, but it had been an uplifting experience which showed how I could use my own problems for the benefit of others.

When I visited Southport during May half term this year I went looking for the family. The mother who had first met me from the lift had returned to Israel that day, but I saw the injured man's wife who told me that he wasn't up for talking. In fact, he wasn't in a good place. He had developed intensive care unit syndrome. Patients recovering from life-threatening conditions in intensive care may also have to battle psychological illness. It's reckoned that between 10% and 20% of such people develop these kinds of problems. Looking at the same four walls each and every day can start playing with the mind. Hearing about the young guy reminded me of how difficult that period of time was when you feel like there is no way out.

Lizzy: *Hannah is unbelievable. The mentoring side of things has given her the chance to see people who are really down and say to them: 'There is hope.'*

CHAPTER TWENTY-FOUR

Routine

'I dream as an able-bodied person.'

You will no doubt share my pleasure in the way that the care system has adapted to my needs in recent months and how it has liberated me in so many ways. However, whatever the system governing me, it does not alter the fact that physically getting through each and every day will always be a struggle. Over the years, I have modified how I do things, but the process is still extremely time-consuming and dependent on a certain amount of knowledge and a huge amount of empathy from those helping me.

The people appointed to look after me have to deal with the most personal of issues, and something that I really want to do before closing this story is to share details with you about my daily routine because I want you to appreciate what goes into achieving what, for you, is probably second nature.

Strangely, my description is going to start last thing at night. There is a reason for this. A day's success definitely depends on the preparation and planning carried out as I get ready for bed the night before. Usually, I'll stay up until about half past eleven and as I guide myself through the kitchen to my bedroom I will start to plan for the next 24 hours. I have to consider everything that I have planned for the next day. Is it a work day? Have I got any appointments? Am I expecting visitors? If I can sort things out the night before I am more likely to be able to get straight up in the morning.

I then have to tick off in my mind the issues which might affect the smooth running of those plans. My catheter is the type that goes straight into my bladder, not like the one I originally had in hospital. It is a more permanent solution and has to be changed every month. I have some medication and a suppository. I try to have my bowels open at night so that in the morning I don't have the worry of it. Crucially important to the planning is the toileting issue, which I find absolutely the hardest thing to deal with because it's the thing that I worry about most. When new carers start I make it very clear that this is a priority area. I don't think that anyone can come into this job unless they are used to personal care. If you find those things uncomfortable you just can't do it. You are, after all, being asked to deal with the most sensitive of issues such as bowel movements.

At the start of the new day I need to be helped into my chair as relaxed as possible so that I can enjoy what's ahead of me and try to have a normal day like anyone else. That's only possible if my carer and I have sorted the toilet situation out and thought it through. I have a bladder washout every evening. It clears any debris. The equipment can be attached to my catheter. It's like a little pouch of liquid which you clip in, then let the liquid out from. It's really straightforward and just like giving medication. I have my leg bag changed every night and emptied throughout the day when needed. It's just for urine. If it fills and isn't emptied the liquid bypasses the catheter and it can be embarrassing and uncomfortable. I worry all the time about smells and having wind. Tia's really funny at work. If I've got a meeting coming up and feel like I've got wind she'll say, 'If you make a noise we'll just pretend it was me!' 99% of the time things run smoothly. Occasionally there might be a bug going round which upsets things, but that can happen to anyone.

I will be fully undressed and have my nightwear put on by the carer on duty before being helped into bed. However, night time is when issues tend to come out, particularly if a lot has happened that day, and there have been many late chats which might go on into the early hours! If I'm at work the next day I have to decide the night before what I want to wear because there is simply no time the following morning to make those agonising decisions that all females face. I'm terrible and I'm sure I drive the carers to distraction at times! I have so many choices and don't decide easily.

There can be days when I'm not working and I'll have up to three changes of outfit before I'm satisfied. Sometimes, I wait for Mum to come back so as not to bother the carers but Mum and Dad get cross at that because it's part of the responsibility that my carers are paid to have. If I want to change my trousers ten times they should be willing to help me.

Before settling down to sleep I will always check the rota to see who will be on duty in the morning when I wake up because I like to call them by name and wish them 'good morning'.

One thing I find hard is not being able to make myself comfortable in bed. Because of that, going to bed is not as pleasurable as it used to be. I rely on someone else to put me in position. If I am not comfortable first time, she will have to move me again and it needs a degree of patience, but people tend to be very good and ask me if I'm absolutely right. I sleep on my side and always insist on sleeping right under my duvet. Once I'm there I cannot move. That can affect my body temperature, which is one of the likeliest causes of a disturbed night. I always sleep with earplugs in because they cut out the perpetual noise of the ventilator in the background and the carers coming in and out for their nightly checks.

The evening carers work from six till midnight, with an overlap period as the next on duty does from eleven at night until half past eight in the morning. They have to observe me regularly through the night and monitor such things as my heart rate. They will come in every hour and do it while I'm asleep. If I need help during the night I will call out but, at times, no one's come in, which is a bit scary. Sometimes, they might be absorbed in something on television. I have my loud signal to attract the carer during the day but can't use it so easily at night because I like to be right under the duvet and I need to blow down a tube to operate it. If there's ever a problem, the last resort would be to wake Mum and Dad who are above me.

I am able to sleep pretty well on the whole but it has taken a long time. I used to have something called chloral hydrate to help me get to sleep. It's a sedative and a hypnotic drug that makes you feel like you are away with the fairies! I first started taking it in Alder Hey, but now I don't need anything. I tend to sleep best after being at work. In fact, I may already have had a nap earlier after returning home.

One thing that fascinates me is that I dream as an able-bodied person but still have the carers in my dreams! In a lot of my dreams I'm unable to get to the toilet in time so subconsciously that must be on my mind a lot. Occasionally, I wake up and think 'I've got people washing and dressing me' and I'm still not fully used to it.

In the morning, the first thing I have to do is take a tablet which protects my gut before I start to eat. I have to wait ten minutes before having some cereal. It might be a bowl of Special K, for instance. I will be fed it on my side because that is the way I have slept. Then there will be other tablets to consume.

For work, it's a half six alarm. If I'm not at work that day I'll not have any need to set an alarm and then will be able to have a lie-in. My carer will open the curtains and let me see what the weather's like. If it's sunny it'll make me get up a bit quicker, maybe around nine o'clock! There could be an appointment to consider and, if so, I'll ask carers to wake me at a particular time.

I'll have my back washed first, then my bottom and the back of my legs. I'm flipped over onto my back, before having my top half washed. My clothes are put on, then it's the same for the lower half of my body. I will be dressed in the way a young child might be dressed although I'm quite flexible for getting my clothes on. When I'm ready to get my trousers pulled up at the back, my sling is slipped under me. I'm lifted off the bed into my chair, then I have my teeth brushed. Normally two people will attend to me. One will clean my teeth, the other will do my hair. They each have their own favourite things to do. Washing, brushing, cleaning, make-up… I appreciate the patience people show. The attitude tends to be, 'If I were doing it for myself I'd want to look good so I understand the need to do it properly for Hannah.' However, one thing I cannot abide is people stopping what they are doing and having a chat! I'm very fussy and want things to be perfect. When you are dependent on others it helps if they can cooperate. I still have days when I'm really down, but things are made a lot easier when you have the right people around you, people who care and don't regard you as a nuisance. Pam, for instance, once took 20 attempts to get my hair as I wanted it. It makes a world of difference when people want to get it just right for you.

I don't like leaving any later than eight for work. Tia comes over the road and is with me by then. We go through Whitegate and I'm usually at work by ten past, quarter past eight. To be honest, it doesn't have to be a specific time of arrival; it's just that I want to get there promptly. That's just how I am.

It's taken me years to sort out a routine. Everything is an effort, but I've worked hard to improve the system. In fact, Mum came down the other day a bit late. She had been tired and struggling to get up. She made the point that I had far more to deal with but still managed to get up quicker than her! That made me smile. Going to university and beginning work have made an early morning routine even more important. Previously, there wasn't any urgency to plan because I didn't have a day to plan for. It was just spent in bed.

After going through that lengthy procedure in a morning, I find it hard to tolerate people who don't understand. Recently I had a chiropody appointment. I had gone through all that I have described and turned up five minutes late. The woman said, 'We're not doing it now.' If she had known the amount of effort it took to get there, she might have reacted differently.

CHAPTER TWENTY-FIVE
The Simple Things in Life
'I miss being by myself.'

How I wish I could do the simple things in life! This can be incredibly frustrating. I watch from my wheelchair as Naomi runs upstairs to put her pyjamas on for a chill-out session in front of the telly. I can't blame her, but what I would give to be able to do that quick change simply and without fuss. That instinctive act, performed without a second's thought by countless people every day, would involve guiding my wheelchair through two doorways and a narrow kitchen to my bedroom, being helped out of it and onto the bed via the hoist, then being undressed before putting my pyjamas on. Then it is back into the chair, again using the hoist, before motoring slowly and carefully past countless obstacles to where I started from. It's so frustrating and really not worth the hassle. Everything is so time-consuming and the simple things that I used to take for granted are beyond me now. I'd love to be able to open the patio door and walk down the garden, but once again, it's like a military operation to get out into the fresh air.

There is no chance to be impromptu, off-the-cuff, flexible or impulsive. Those days have gone and it hurts. How nice it would be to be able to suddenly change my plans in a moment. Spontaneity, sadly, goes out of the window. I can't just wake up one morning and say to myself, 'I'm going to have a day off work.' I have to plan that decision in advance. If I'm working I've got to have the carers there to help me get up. The night and morning persons will get me ready if I'm going to work, but if I'm not going to work I'll need two daytime carers; I don't really want to be getting up at seven o' clock in the morning if I'm not going to work, so two will be needed to help me dress later.

I miss being by myself. It would be lovely to be able to sit, or preferably lounge, in front of the television and tuck into a box of chocolates one-by-one! I can have the telly and the chocolates but they cannot reach my mouth without someone feeding them to me. Once again, that instinctive, guilty, solitary pleasure has gone. In fact, I know that I'll never be by myself again and the chance to do what I want when I want has passed me by. I would love to take Bella for a walk by myself without having to be manoeuvred into the back of the car, clamped in, driven to the walk then accompanied as I go round. I've learnt to negotiate most obstacles and tight spaces in my electric wheelchair and I can call Bella to me but would love to throw her a stick myself. I can see her diving ungraciously into the river and swimming to the stick but it has been thrown there by someone else. How I wish that I could do that myself. I would even settle for dealing with the poo bag! That's an enormous thing for me to say and do.

There always has to be someone around to help me and, as such, I have lost the independence that is an important part of normal everyday life. Yes, it has returned to a degree with the freedom provided by the personalised care but what I have now will never replace what I would have had because my life is controlled. What I yearn for is something that I know many others just take for granted, but when you've lost that ability to 'do it yourself' you really notice it. The harsh reality is that I can't do anything in private again and my emotions are always bared for all to see. If I'm happy everyone knows I'm happy, if I'm upset everyone knows I'm upset. If I want to cry, the only time I can do that is in private when I'm in my bed with a duvet over me. It tends to be at night when I get upset. However, it's not as often as I used to.

Every step has been daunting, but I have reached many of my targets and I am proud of myself for doing that. When I started to rebuild my life I thought that everything that I wanted was beyond me. I was not prepared to admit that I would be able to achieve anything. I told others on many occasions in the early days that there was nothing to aim for. There was no way that

I was going to go there, do this or try that. Well, I have proved myself wrong and, in a strange sort of way, my determination has been the trigger to enable me to achieve more than many able-bodied people. There will be many more achievements to come. A lot of it is down to having a positive mental attitude and strength of mind. It is a challenge, don't get me wrong, but one thing leads to another and I have constantly surprised myself. One thing that illustrates this perfectly is going abroad for a holiday.

CHAPTER TWENTY-SIX
Holiday Time

'Mum took the orders, turned round and walked straight into the pool!'

We had some lovely family holidays before my illness, but what had happened to me had cast doubts over whether we could achieve that same happiness again, particularly overseas. There had already been some success in Britain since my illness, but planning for abroad was a whole different ball game, particularly because it involved air travel. I remember pestering Mum and Dad constantly about when we could go abroad, but this would not be like any other holiday preparation! My dad gets so stressed about having everything packed for an ordinary trip out down the road, so you can imagine his concern magnified multiple times.

Despite all that, Mum and Dad found a hotel in Tenerife which looked as if it had everything to meet the needs of a disabled young woman and her family. I could not wait to get there and knew that the Canary Islands could always be guaranteed to have plenty of sunshine. There were plenty of positive pictures coming into my mind, but I must admit that I was scared about the plane journey. I was first on, which was a good start because I didn't want to be last and have everyone staring at me. It would be so embarrassing! The stewardesses took me out of my wheelchair and put me on this narrow chair which fitted down the aisle. They were really nice and explained how everything worked. Some disabled travellers have a harness fitted to the chair, but I couldn't be bothered. I was really nervous as the time for departure drew closer and asked Mum to hold my hand at take-off. It was a really strange experience leaving the ground as a tetraplegic. I needed that harness after all as I slipped forward dramatically and almost out of my seat! Anyway, I recovered and must have struck a chord with it being my first such flight because the cabin crew brought us a bottle of champagne and glasses for the family! How nice was that? Tenerife's a long flight at the best of times but particularly so when you are disabled. You are tightly bound and uncomfortable and when we landed my body flew forward again!

We got a taxi to the hotel. It was really good to be in Tenerife and brilliant to be back abroad. I couldn't wait to soak up the sun! Naomi was already on the island with her friends and we met up with her. We did loads of things, including going into the swimming pool. There was a hoist at the side. I was lifted into the seat, which swung over the pool and lowered me in. I loved it!

A brilliantly funny thing happened on the second day. We were by the pool enjoying the sun when Mum asked if anyone wanted an ice cream. She had just been to the shops and was still fully clothed. She took the orders, turned round and walked straight into the pool! The funniest thing was that she just kept walking through the water and out on the other side with the ice cream money still in her hand! We were all laughing so much. It was definitely the highlight of the holiday.

The package was all-inclusive so we ate in the hotel which was in the resort of Los Christianos. We also managed to go out a few times during the stay. It wasn't ideal because I was in my manual chair and had to be pushed each time. One day we visited the market and knowing me, of course, we managed to find a few clothes shops! It was ideal for a first holiday away. We were there for a week and we went the year after as well. There was a lovely lady called Magdalena and she put me to bed and dressed me in the morning. I'm still in contact with her although she's now living in Austria. She sends me Christmas and birthday cards.

Because the holiday went so well it made us think, as a family, that we should just get on and do things. We rented a specially adapted villa in Spain. It was a good place, but I found the intense heat very difficult and there was no air conditioning. There was a pool, however, and I was able to cool down in that because, as in Tenerife, it was designed with a hoist to lower disabled people into the water. The family in charge of the villa were really nice. They cooked us a gorgeous paella one night!

For a change, we visited Euro Disney in Paris one year and were able to go in the van with Eurostar. This meant that we could include my electric wheelchair in the plans. It had always been too risky by plane because if anything went wrong the chair couldn't be replaced. We had about four nights near Paris, without Jess on this occasion. We took the hoist and mattress and stayed in the Davy Crockett Ranches, about a 15-minute drive from the Disneyland parks. The ranches weren't specifically for disabled people. I missed the sunshine of Tenerife and Spain, but Disney was very welcoming and disabled-friendly. I could also go on a number of rides and visit some shows which made me feel that I was included. It did not compare to Disney World in Florida, which we had visited as a family before I became ill. The American site was much bigger and also a lot hotter! However, we had a nice time.

Next stop was Portugal, not far from Vilamoura. It was in a lovely little village which was not touristy. The villa where we stayed was situated on a hill with a lovely garden and its own pool. It couldn't have been more perfect. The man who owned the villa was actually a tetraplegic himself, having sustained a spinal injury from playing rugby. He had met his wife when she was a spinal-injuries nurse. They had kitted out this holiday villa especially for people with disabilities. They also lived in it, on the top floor. They were called Denise and Simon and I am still friends with them on Facebook. Denise's help took a lot of pressure off Mum and Dad. Another bonus was that the couple had their own van which allowed us to travel. It meant that we could do things like we used to, even allowing for my disability. We went to some of the surrounding towns and, of course, down to the seaside. We have now been to Portugal twice.

I must tell you about the first holiday that I spent away without Mum and Dad. You've got to hear about this! It was back in the days before the personalised health care package came into operation. Mum had seen an advert for the Calvert

Trust, based in Keswick in the Lake District. It specialised in providing holidays for disabled people, giving them the chance to do outdoor activities. Four carers went with me, led by Chris. She is a lovely lady who I always feel comfortable with. She was also known to Mum because Chris was having her daughter in hospital about the same time that Mum was expecting me.

The Back-Up Trust charity offers visits to the Calvert Trust. Mum thought she was booking me on that, but in fact she mistakenly arranged for something quite different. It turned out that it wasn't just for people with spinal injuries but for those with all kinds of disabilities, both mental and physical. Some had Alzheimer's disease. Activities started at eight in the morning, by which time you were expected to have had breakfast. I was inconvenienced by a pressure sore at this time so we had to organise local district nurses to come in and dress it.

On arrival I got put in a group and we went to a gym where they said, 'Let's play a game. We're going to throw a ball and when you catch the ball you have to say what your name is.' What chance had I of catching a ball? It suddenly dawned on me what I had agreed to do. I burst into tears and went into the toilet with Chris. I cried my eyes out and told her that I wanted to go home. Chris suggested that I give it a chance, but it felt like being homesick on a school trip.

I took Chris's advice, stuck at it and set off on more activities. I was in a group with a guy whose male carer quickly took a shine to me, and this was to ruin the whole holiday because he kind of stalked me! We stayed in the same group for every activity and he always wanted to pair up with me. He soon discovered where I lived and was delighted to learn that I was only about 20 minutes from him as he came from Runcorn. He kept buying me things, including ten CDs of bands like Led Zeppelin – more the sort of thing my dad likes!

The venue was excellent and the course had plenty going for it, but it wasn't ideal for my needs. There were things like archery, which I obviously had no chance of doing, but I did go on the pony and trap which was really good. You could put the chair on a special cart. Less pleasurable was abseiling. I used a harness but hated it! It was a real out-of-body experience for me because I couldn't feel where my body was ending. All I could feel was a head! I went sailing and was lifted into the boat in my chair.

I had not insisted that I leave early and go home but I was homesick throughout and my carers were finding it hard because, as I was so unsettled, they were getting little sleep. The 'holiday' was from Monday to Friday but, in reality, it felt like longer. I rang home each night complaining about what I had been put on. As I had come by myself there was no one else I could relate to easily on the trip and spend spare time with. Consequently, I preferred to be in my room with the carers watching television such as *Coronation Street*.

The set-up and arrangements for all the activities were good but for me, personally, it was a disaster and my mum and dad felt guilty about what they had sent me on. I just didn't feel able to cope with what was on offer. Now I would actually look forward to something like that because I've changed and moved on. I'd be ready and determined to do it in a way that I clearly wasn't capable of back then.

After we had returned the attentive carer came across one of my carers who lived in Runcorn. She was out shopping and when she came back to her car the pictures of the holiday were stuffed under the windscreen wiper!

It wasn't the only time that I attracted unwanted attention. There was an ambulance journey to Southport which I had to share with a guy of about 60 who drove me absolutely nuts. We had to pick him up, coincidentally, from Runcorn! He was really weird. He kept saying things like, 'You've got lovely eyes' and 'I love your make-up'! It was really freaky and unsettling. Anyway, I am in danger of going off-subject... again!

We have had some good holidays since I became ill. It is so important that everyone gets a holiday, not just me. It is also nice to have some time on our own without carers and personal assistants. It gives us time to chuckle, laugh and argue with each other. All of us have had to cope with the influx of carers and personal assistants into our hallowed space and it makes it all the more special when we can spend time together just as a family. Unfortunately, we did not get away in 2011 because I wasn't well, but we were to make up for that in 2012!

CHAPTER TWENTY-SEVEN
France 2012

'We did the kinds of visits we used to do as a family.'

My summer holiday in 2012 was just one of the best I've had. I have already explained about the troubled period leading up to it, but it was soon forgotten as Mum, Dad, Jess, Naomi and I had the most amazing time in Normandy. It was the first time we had gone away and been able to do the sorts of things that we had done years ago. It was so lovely that I didn't want to come home! Jess, Naomi and I got on really well.

I was so organised before we went and took the least stuff out of anybody. Dad managed to get a roof box for the car, which was good. As I was going on a ferry I could take the electric wheelchair. That was important for my independence because I just hate being pushed around by others. Dad was typically nervous about taking the chair in case it broke but my view was to take the risk. If the worst came to the worst we'd just have to stay in our accommodation. It was the first time I'd been on a ferry for 15 years or so. Dad had been a bit off-putting, going on about seasickness, but he didn't bother me at all.

The place we went to had about five gîtes all clustered together with a courtyard in the middle. The weather was so hot, which of course suited me! There were rabbits and guinea pigs running around. The man who owned the site was called Rob. He was from Oldham and his wife, Melanie, was French. They were so laid back and nice people. They also had about five dogs and five cats so Naomi was in her element! She could pick the cats up as well, which was a bonus. We hired a hoist for me, which was a big help. I just had to take the ventilator, the suction and the medication I needed.

There were so many things to do. I loved looking round the local markets and we visited the Bayeux Tapestry, which was nearby. It is an embroidered cloth about 70 metres long which shows the events leading up to the Norman conquest of England and was really interesting to see after I'd heard and read about it so many times at school.

We got up and went to bed when we wanted. Melanie helped me get up in the morning with Mum. Jess and Naomi made me look nice each day while Dad cooked every night after we'd been to the supermarket. That was another nice thing. In the old days, when we went to EuroCamp, Dad used to do all the barbecues. We played games and had a laugh. It was so nice, in fact, that I honestly didn't miss television, and that's a big thing for me to admit to!

We went to a Flunch near the ferry on the way back. For those of you who have never heard of Flunch, it is a fast-food restaurant and there are about 200 of them across France. We were about to drive past, then saw it. I said, 'We can't get back on the ferry without going to a Flunch again!' We used to go to Flunch when we were little. I must admit, though, that it didn't live up to expectations. I was really disappointed that we didn't get a child's gift like we used to!

The only downside was a rough crossing on the way back. When we got on they had the cars really tightly packed together. I had to guide my wheelchair past, telling a watchful Dad all the time, 'Don't you *dare* tell me how to drive this wheelchair!' Once we started sailing I just sat there perfectly happy and unaffected. I kept thinking that this was a better way to travel than on a plane, but I doubt whether some of the others agreed by the time we arrived back in England!

We've booked again for next year, but this time a place for 14 which will give us more options for who to take. The holiday was a reminder that I can still have a really nice time.

CHAPTER TWENTY-EIGHT
The Future

'I want a bungalow with my own garden.'

What has the future got in store for me? Well, I know what I can say for sure.

I know that...

> ... I will require physical support for the rest of my life.
> ... I will have regular visits to hospitals.
> ... I will be on daily medication.
> ... My ventilator will be a constant companion.
> ... Every day will need to be organised with military precision.

Beyond those restrictions, I have learned and achieved enough to know that I need not fear the future. I have grown in confidence and matured as a person and there is so much more that I know I can achieve. I am eager to develop some of the opportunities that have recently come my way and with the love and support of family and friends anything is possible.

My ultimate goal is to meet somebody, live independently and have a family. I'll make no bones about it – I will be disappointed with life if that doesn't happen to me. It's a scary prospect which I cannot take in at the moment but one day... Hopefully it will happen, but I've just got to accept that I'm going to take longer than most.

One of the absolute key issues is if or when I should decide to leave home and live by myself. Andy's got his own place and that's something that I would like to achieve for myself eventually. I keep picturing what it might look like in my mind. I know that I can survive in practical terms because I've always got the help from my carers. I've started to show that I don't need my mum and dad to be there all the time.

Mentally, it will be a much bigger step. Setting up by myself would make me really nervous, but I want to do it someday. It would be a huge wrench because, despite all the difficulties faced at home since I left hospital, I have always seen it as a very special place. I love family life and having my loved ones around me. It's brilliant having Naomi living at home at the moment.

On the rare occasions that my mum and dad have gone away since my illness I've missed both of them loads. This house will always be my home even when I'm no longer in it. In these rooms I've shared so many Christmases, parties and laughter. I would be sad to move but people do it. I'll still be driven up and down Chester Road and think, 'That is my house.' I love having a busy house as well, which makes staying at home an advantage.

I want a bungalow with my own garden. When it happens it won't be a normal move like Jess's. It won't be like it should have been. I would have to have a little intercom for when people come to the front door. Dad said, 'You know the road off Riddings Lane, the one with the old-age pensioner assisted housing? You can go there.' I replied, 'I'm not moving there! I'm not 90!' It's got little cul-de-sacs with tiny houses full of old people. Thanks, Dad! Despite that, Hartford would be really nice and one thing is for certain: I would need to end up near to the family home.

> **Fran:** *The ideal would be to have Hannah living up the road in her own place. She tries her best but worries so much and wants to please. She is hypersensitive and it all adds to the pressure of the situation. Hannah's vulnerability is scary. She is surrounded by lovely people everywhere at the moment but to transfer that to independent living is something else. You have to have utmost trust.*

I know that when it happens it's going to be a big period of change. My friend Sarah was talking to me about it the other day; she is thinking the same way. She said, 'If I ever move out of home will you promise me that you'll come round for tea one night a week?' It was as if she wanted reassurance that she wouldn't be lonely. She lives in a busy house, like I do. Even though I love having people around me I would also love my own space.

> **Helen:** *Hannah visited my house in Manchester. It's a new build with wide doorways and a path right up to the front and back doors with no step to negotiate. She got her wheelchair around really easily, which pleased her. I think that it helped her to realise that she could go it alone in the right surroundings. She said that she would like something similar.*

We'll see how things pan out over the coming years and then maybe I can persuade Dave and Sue to write volume two!

CHAPTER TWENTY-NINE
A Standing Ovation
'Hannah has moved and inspired me.'

You will remember the talk that I referred to in the introduction of this book. It was such an important day in my life that I want to tell you more about it. I had been invited to address a group of health professionals comprising nurses, doctors and the like at St John's Church in Hartford. The subject was 'Personalised Health Budgets'. When I got the agenda it had written on it, 'Hannah Rose: welcome to my world'!

I discussed it with Dad and we decided to start with some pictures of me before I was ill. I explained about going from being able to doing everything myself to being restricted by my illness. Dad helped me complete a PowerPoint presentation. I was really nervous! In fact, my nerves built up so much that Mum even suggested I pull out rather than work myself up. I had promised, though, and didn't want to let the group down.

My personal assistant, Kate, and Dad went with me. Kate's job was to help me present the talk. She was as nervous as I was! Dad had told me to get up really early so that Kate and I could do a run-through of the presentation with him. We fulfilled our side of the bargain, but Dad was nowhere to be seen! He was upstairs and presumably asleep because we could not rouse him. He had the PowerPoint with him as well! We shouted and rang him without success. Five minutes before we were due to leave one of the carers had to bang loudly on his bedroom door. He had indeed overslept and was very apologetic! This was something I could have done without. To make matters slightly worse, his car was blocking our exit!

Although I wasn't on until the afternoon I wanted to get to the hall for a morning session which sounded really interesting. *Big Gary's House*, based on a real-life case study, was a comic sketch that told the story of a person's disability and experiences with various services. It was really good and took my mind off what was to come in the afternoon. Lunch followed, then me!

There were about 80 people in the hall. Once I started, I began to really enjoy it. The presentation took about 25 minutes. The slides included pictures of me before and after the illness. As the sequence unfolded I gathered more confidence and started to ad-lib. One picture taken some years ago showed Alison and her son, Ryan. I came off script and said, 'Look at that young lad. He's going to high school now!' Another picture showed me and my friends clubbing.

The presentation was meant to be positive, showing how my personalised health budget had helped me cope. Although I mentioned certain issues such as the bureaucracy that we constantly faced with the old system I was always tactful. In fact, there were members of Complex Care in the audience. Key to my presentation was the message that services need to change to adapt to each individual as their needs change.

I did not have to worry about how well the talk had been received because, as I finished, I was given a standing ovation. I had a beaming smile from ear to ear!

The presentation was followed by a question and answer session. I was on safe ground with the first question; someone asked me where I got my hair done! Then there was one from my disabled friend Andy, who had made the effort to come and listen to me. He asked me, 'What's your next step, Hannah?' My answer? 'To move out and set up home by myself.'

What Andy said next really shocked me. He turned to the audience and said, 'Everybody, I want you to know how much Hannah has moved and inspired me over the last few years.' He was close to tears.

It had been the most wonderful experience and I thought that I should have invited all my personal assistants, but if it hadn't have gone so well I would have been annoyed for showing myself up in front of them. Another regret was that I wished that I'd recorded it. Dad got his camera out at one point but I was in such stress after the morning we'd had that I told him to put it away. Never mind! A success it was, though, and I've now been asked to cover the other half of Cheshire, somewhere on the Wirral.

> *Jessica: It will be wonderful if Hannah can make this package work and put a model in place that can be rolled out to other people. There are plenty of others who are going to be in her position in the future but perhaps not as well off in that they won't have the support network that Hannah has or Hannah's intelligence and confidence. Everyone knows their place in the system and what they have to do to make it work.*

Some weeks later, I was approached by the University of Chester and asked to give a lecture on rehabilitation to their Health and Social Care students. It was all about gaining independence.

There was an embarrassing moment when the lecturer helped me set up my PowerPoint because the M & S shopping page came up on the large screen! It clearly indicated what I had been doing last night, but it started things off with a smile. I had the whole morning allocated to me so started by talking about myself for an hour or so and after a short break, I gave them a planned exercise where I went through my daily routine and got the students to identify which aspects were connected with health and which with social issues. Afterwards, they said that they really appreciated it because it made them realise how much they take for granted.

CONCLUSION

I am always going to think how unfair life is and be sad about what has happened to me. To be struck in such a way at a time when your life, personality and character are all blossoming is cruel. I've been cheated out of my formative years when everything should have been exciting and new.

Countless thoughts have gone through my mind over the last 13 years as I have experienced the massive range of emotions from dejection to euphoria. Becoming trapped by thought is something that can happen all too easily when you are lying or sitting still all the time.

Negative thinking has often led me to wonder, 'What have I done wrong to be punished in this way?' Before my illness I worried constantly, almost obsessively. I worried about school, exams, relationships and much more besides. I have often thought that someone has been looking down, saying to me, 'If you're going to worry about all that then you can start to worry about this. Wham!'

Then I have thought, 'Maybe I was going to do something really bad with my life, because I couldn't cope with what it threw at me, and this has stopped me from doing it.' I used to worry about sharing toilets at school. Maybe someone up there was thinking, 'Right, you are going to go from one extreme to the other. Now you won't be able to use the toilet.'

I still worry about everything. I even worry about the fact that I worry! I wish I didn't worry so much about other people and what they think of me. This particularly frustrates Dad and Jess, not Mum so much because she is more like me. I've felt a bit ashamed of myself because too often I've worried about making sure everything is right with the carers when I should have concerned myself more with the needs of my family. I need to put my life into perspective. I've not chosen this for myself. Other people can walk away from situations in a way that I cannot, so why am I wasting so much time and effort worrying about them? This is one of my biggest problems.

If I could have had a crystal ball and foreseen that I was going to be ill, would it have been better to have known in advance? Imagine... At some point in the future you will have to breathe with the aid of a machine, you won't be able to walk, you won't be able to go to the toilet, you won't ever be by yourself and you're going to have to rely on everybody around you. What would my reaction have been? Would I have then thrown myself into loads of other things to make the most of the time that I had left to enjoy them?

I watched an edition of *DIY SOS* on television. It featured a makeover for a person with motor neurone disease. His family knew that his life was limited and that he would die all too soon. I thought to myself how I had had some bad luck but that things could be worse. I got so upset for this guy and it made me cry. My dad couldn't understand me! It must be so difficult if you have a degenerative illness. If you are young and know what's going to happen it must be even more difficult. At least my condition will remain constant and I can do some planning towards what I want to achieve through the rest of my life.

There is definitely a flip-side where I can marvel at what I have done as a disabled person. I would even argue that I am now the most confident that I have ever been, perhaps even too confident at times! This might sound strange, but I don't know if I'd be as confident now if I hadn't been ill. I definitely think that university helped because it made me go out and make new friends. The same can be said for work.

As the years have passed, and despite the continued dips, there have definitely been more good days and the positive, forward-looking, ambitious side of me has taken a greater hold. Christopher Reeve, alias Superman, became a quadriplegic after being thrown from a horse in 1995. He has since inspired many with his words and actions and one of his most powerful quotes was, 'Once you choose hope anything is possible'. Since those first GCSE results showed what could be achieved – and

I'm sure that those three grades gave me more pleasure than the 'normal' eight or nine expected of an able-bodied Hannah – I have been immensely proud of what I have done. There will be more dark hours, I am sure, but, equally, there are likely to be longer periods of light in between and I am determined to make the most of my situation.

I don't even care if people stare at me now. I just smile back at them. When I first became ill I said to Dad, 'I'm never going to shop in Northwich or eat in a restaurant. There's no way that I will go out anywhere.' In fact, I had a massive argument with him on one occasion about it. I had read a letter which I'd been sent in which someone who had had an accident had written, 'I know at first you won't want to do normal things again but in time you will.' I said to Dad, 'No way! That's him, that's how he feels, but I definitely won't feel the same way. No one in Hartford, Northwich or anywhere is going to see me looking like this.'

Time alters our perspective and I go into shops and restaurants without hesitation. I will ask someone to take an item off the shelf for me so that I can have a closer look. I'm happy to try something on in full view in the middle of a shop. I can go out in my electric wheelchair and talk freely to people without worrying that they are looking at me and thinking 'disabled', although I'm still at pains to make them aware that it has not always been this way.

One of the most important messages which I am hoping will come out of this book is that things do change and, in time, you develop the confidence to move on. I want people to realise that. It's not easy, nor does it happen overnight, but there is *always* a way through despite the apparently insurmountable problems that might lie ahead for any of us. I cannot believe how much I have achieved over the last 13 years. From time to time I come across fellow disabled people who are, for whatever reason, unable to contemplate ever having any sense of purpose to look forward to in their lives. I try to get across to them that they can move on, but at the same time, I understand if they find it impossible to relate to me. After all, I was there myself. Their plight takes me back to where I was in the early years of my illness and it makes me realise how far I have come.

It's important that I have those opportunities to reflect because they make it crystal clear to me how I have defied the odds and made something of my life.

Philosophically I have pondered the question, 'If I were just normal and had gone to university and got a job in the normal way, what would I have done? How would life have panned out?' There's no doubt in my mind that I have achieved and experienced things as a disabled person that I would not have achieved as an able-bodied person. The intensity of some of the experiences and emotions could never have been replicated in a 'normal' existence.

Going into Alder Hey seems both relatively new and yet an age ago. When I'm telling people what happened to me I don't like it to come across as dramatic but the fact of the matter is that it was! Listening to my family as we created this book gave me the chance to learn so much more about what happened all those years ago and made me realise how horrific the whole thing was. The exercise has given me a whole new view on my illness and my recovery.

Ultimately, I think this book will prove to have been a good thing because it will make people realise what an impact it's all had on our family. I could not have got to where I am today without their love, support and inspiration. It has been difficult for all of them, both collectively and individually. I feel for my sisters, Jess and Naomi, who have had to cope with the attention and time that has inevitably gone my way. They have sacrificed a lot over the years and it must have been frustrating and difficult for them.

I don't know how Mum and Dad have coped without cracking up. No two humans could have done more. It is something that would have broken many a relationship, but they are still here for me. Mum's friend Alex came round the other week with her new baby daughter. It was Alex's first child and it was strange to see Mum holding her. Alex was so excited and it made me think that Mum had once been like that with me, excitedly holding her first child. It must hurt her so much with everything that's happened to me. She cannot change anything, though. What has happened has happened.

I want to do as many of the things that I would have done had I not been struck down by illness. Physically I have changed and that has placed its demands on me, but spiritually and emotionally, after all I have been through, I remain the same Hannah deep down. I still love fashion, television and celebrity, I still worry more than I should do, I still listen in to other conversations when I shouldn't and I still like to have a good time! Just as my name is spelt the same both ways so I have remained the same person both ways, able-bodied and disabled.

I am proud of what I have achieved and ready to move on. Whatever I do in the future, I want to continue to make a mark on life. I'll let you know how I get on!

Thanks for the Memory...

Since finishing this book I have lost my very special friend, Bella. She was eleven years old and not well by the end. On the last night, I sat up by myself with her. I talked about old times and made Bella aware of how much I loved her. Mum and Dad took over nursing duties from midnight until about half past two in the morning when Alison told them to go to bed. Alison was still on duty when Bella finally passed away at around four o'clock in the morning. It was fitting that she was there because Alison is the only carer left who was with us when Bella first arrived. Alison crept upstairs and gave Mum and Dad the news and I heard from Mum when I woke about eight. Just for good measure, Alison rang later to tell me that it had been a peaceful ending.